EVIL,
GOOD
AND
BEYOND

Dados Internacionais de Catalogação na Publicação (CIP)
(Câmara Brasileira do Livro, SP, Brasil)

Gikovate, Flávio
   Evil, good and beyond : the selfish, the generous and the
fair / Flávio Gikovate ; [translation Alison Entrekin]. – São Paulo :
MG Editores, 2009.
   Título original: O mal, o bem e mais além : egoístas, generosos
e justos.

   Bibliografia.
   ISBN 978-85-7255-062-8

   1. Bem e mal 2. Casais 3. Comportamento humano 4. Ética
5. Relações interpessoais I. Título.

09-06211   CDD-158.24

          Índice para catálogo sistemático:

      1. Bem e mal : Casais : Relações interpessoais :
          Psicologia aplicada   158.24

EVIL, GOOD AND BEYOND

the selfish, the generous and the fair

Flávio Gikovate

Translated by Alison Entrekin

MG EDITORES

Translation: **Alison Entrekin**
Cover design: **Alberto Mateus**
Art and design: **Crayon Editorial**

MG Editores
Editorial departament:
Rua Itapicuru, 613 – 7º andar
05006-000 – São Paulo – SP
Brazil
Tel.: (55) (11) 3872-3322
Fax: (55) (11) 3872-7476
http://www.mgeditores.com.br
e-mail: mg@mgeditores.com.br

Printed in Brazil

Introduction

My reflections on morality began in the second half of the 1970's. I had begun to detect certain characteristics in my analyses of what brought couples together. The frequency with which psychological opposites were attracted to one another impressed me precisely because it was completely out of keeping with probabilistic forecasts. Almost all quieter, relatively nonaggressive sorts married extroverts with "strong personalities". And they continue to do so.

In 1977 I published the book *Você é feliz?* (*Are You Happy?*), in which I described more selfish people in detail. At the time people were beginning to speculate about the "Era of Narcissism", in which it was apparently OK to free oneself of all kinds of inner limits and live according to one's desires. I never shared this point of view, because I saw selfishness as a moral flaw. I believed generosity was a virtue and selfishness, a vice. That's how all the "nice folks" thought.

In 1981 I published *Em busca da felicidade* (*In Search of Happiness*), in which I emphatically aired my early doubts about the "purity" of generous behaviour. I was beginning to tune into the strong presence of vanity and certain aspects of the power play between generous and selfish types, who have always been intensely attracted to one another.

I have worked with thousands of patients and meditated a lot on the subject, which, throughout these decades, has always proved an important factor in the choice of romantic partner, as well as a basic element in the difficulties that arise in intimate relationships. Additionally, I have studied the ways in which sexuality manifests in these two types of human beings. Moral issues have thus always been present in my books.

I have often been labelled as Manichaean, as someone who only sees things in black and white, incapable of understanding that we are complex creatures. I think the reasons for this criticism reside, above all, in my own expressive limitations. We aren't always able to put what we think into words. I believe I have made important progress in this area, both in writing and in speaking to a wide range of audiences.

I also believe that people's willingness to consider my hypotheses and thoughts on morality has changed. I am better able to express myself, but people are also reading with less resistance! When I started to write about these issues, Brazil was living under a military dictatorship. There were those who were opposed to it — the "good guys" — and those who supported it — the "bad guys". It was impossible to try to convince people that the "good guys" weren't so good after all. There was the Berlin Wall: those on this side of the wall thought that "evil" resided on the other side, and vice-versa. In addition to the cultural tradition in which we were raised, which has always held generosity as a virtue, we lived in a divided world, in which taking sides seemed imperative.

Today this has all changed, and only a few people still believe in "axes of good and evil". Perhaps it is time to revisit, without bias (free of the prejudices that constitute our beliefs, and paying closer attention to the facts than to ideology), the values that are going to guide us from here on. We have been living in a vacuum, without references and anchorage in our moments of greatest suffering. This might explain why depression is becoming more and more commonplace.

It is not my intention — nor am I equipped — to exhaustively examine such a complex subject, which perhaps should be revisited from time to time. The book you are about to read is an overview of everything I have managed to understand about morality seen through the prism my profession has provided me. If it serves as inspiration and a springboard for all of us to concern ourselves with building a set of values to guide us on this planet we have changed so radically, I will have fulfilled what I set out to do.

Flávio Gikovate
April 2005

Evil, Good and Beyond

one

I recently read a review of a book published in the United States called *Evil: An Investigation*[1]. The author of the review was critical of it, among other reasons, because it didn't make a significant contribution to solving the problem at hand; in other words, it didn't put forward any worthwhile hypotheses about the origin of "evil". Nor did the critic, in turn, consider himself capable of answering such a complex, difficult question, despite his considerable qualifications. This prompted me to write a new text dealing with my own reflections on a subject I have been mulling over since 1977.

Reading this interesting critical text (and others), I learned that "good" and "evil" are not actual entities. They are constructions, almost myths, which have been developing for millenniums and have, in a way, formed a dichotomy seen as inevitable. God and the Devil have fought and will go on fighting forever! As such, "good" looks to "evil" for definition and existence, just as "evil" is defined in comparison with "good". Most people believe this duality describes us to a T; that we essentially

1 Lance Morrow, *Evil: An Investigation*, New York: Basic Books, 2003. Review by Philip Cole in *Radical Philosophy*, issue 126, July 2004.

belong to two opposing factions, not just morally, but in everything: Yin and Yang.

My concern with this essential issue has grown over the years. It arose spontaneously and unexpectedly in my analysis of how human relationships are established, especially marital ties between men and women. **What has always surprised me is the fact that the overwhelming majority of "voluntary" choices — those which take place spontaneously and are attributed to romantic love — repeat a single pattern: people who are very different to one another, opposites in certain essential aspects of their personalities, are drawn to one another.** I was also intrigued by the fact that people seemed to consider it the natural order of things. In other words, the coming together of opposites was encouraged — as registered in nursery rhymes such as "Jack Sprat could eat no fat / his wife could eat no lean / and so betwixt the two of them / they licked the platter clean" and popular expressions such as "opposites attract". Freud's reflections in *On Narcissism: An Introduction* (1914) also took this path, suggesting that the most sophisticated thing, from a psychological point of view, was to seek in others whatever we were lacking, instead of seeking an affinity based on "narcissistic identification". In other words, people who were shy, discreet, passive, and who found it hard to stand up for themselves should marry people who were outgoing, bold, aggressive, and demanding.

The uniting of opposites was defined and built upon

the existence of two opposing types of human beings. Additionally, any romantic interest between them seemed to validate these types. This hasn't changed, because even today sentimental choices are made in this manner, reflecting a societal belief in two acceptable modes of human behaviour, regardless of their antagonism. We can either be extroverted or introverted. We can keep our aggression in check or have a "short fuse". We can have stable moods and points of view or we can be unstable and unpredictable. And so on.

2
two

We tend to assume that difference automatically means hierarchy. If there are two different personality types, then one must be superior to the other. If men and women are different, then one is superior and the other, inferior. The criteria used to define this depend on the observer and his or her position of power. Certain observations are accepted by the majority and become engrained social values that remain practically unquestioned for generations. It doesn't guarantee, however, the veracity of the established hierarchy. This was the case with the age-old belief in male "superiority", debunked in more recent times, and with good reason.

At this point in my musings I found myself facing my first conundrum and source of controversy. If we take as true my decades-old theory that love is born of admiration, then love between opposites implies that we must admire our opposites. In other words, impulsive sorts admire those who show more control (therefore, superior), while controlled sorts tend to admire those who are impulsive. How, then, can we say that one type is superior?

Words like "good" and "bad", "right" and "wrong" don't seem terribly useful in an objective assessment of personality types. These constructions, which imply pre-existing value judgments, can undermine an evaluation intended to be as objective as possible — but which will never be a hundred percent. **Hasty value-judgements are not useful when trying to understand the human condition.** Ideally we should try to suspend judgement for as long as possible during the process of analysis. **Eventually, however, moral assessment is inevitable, at which point we should face it fearlessly and without reservation.** But before this we need to try to observe our peers as we do other mammals, and describe their behaviour without bias. This is almost impossible, but it is what we should aim for, despite the difficulty.

In psychology we can employ several other criteria for evaluating people, to establish which personality types and behaviours are more sophisticated than others. Sophistication might be, for example, a person's ability to refrain from behaviours typical of young children, which are, in a sense, part of the way we are by nature. We refer to the impulsive, even aggressive behaviour typical of children when they are denied something as immature — and the word contains a value-judgement. Immaturity means unsophisticated behaviour that has not been perfected and polished. **As a rule, we are born with less tolerance than we need for the trials and tribulations of life in society.**

I believe it is no exaggeration to say that low frustration tolerance can stunt a child's emotional development. It is an inability to overcome a *biological* limitation in order to meet a *cultural* requirement of the society in which we live. This is the most striking characteristic of emotional immaturity, which perpetuates itself precisely because it interrupts a person's process of adapting to his or her social world. Something is missing for these people, who reach adulthood still unable to cope effectively with life's inevitable pain.

Children who don't learn to deal better with suffering — this is not about enjoying suffering, much less looking for it; rather it is being able to deal well with the suffering that life inexorably dishes up — interrupt another extremely important process, which is learning to put themselves in other people's shoes. This ability to step outside of ourselves and imagine ourselves in someone else's situation comes with the sophistication of reason[1]. When we reach a particular level of functional development we are able to leave the concrete world of facts and enter the realm of that which doesn't exist — the world of the imagination. When we put ourselves in another person's shoes we try to see the world from their point of view, which shatters our exclusively egocentric vision. We acquire the ability to imagine what the next person is feeling, which mostly means being able to imagine their suffering. Children who don't cope well with psychological pain tend to interrupt this process of putting themselves in other people's shoes, since it generates new suffering, now felt vicariously. They will be limited to a simplistic, egocentric view of life. They will also be unable to fully develop morally, since putting oneself in someone else's shoes means considering other points of view and the rights of others.

If we take this one step further and consider that low frustration tolerance is not only immature but also weak, we can then begin the dissection needed to tackle the complex question at hand. The term "weak" contains more moral judgment than "immaturity". These two words can be compared to their opposites, seen as hierarchically superior, or more appropriate. Maturity is understood as superior to immaturity, and strength superior to weakness.

Maturity is superior to immaturity because those who are better able to tolerate obstacles are better prepared for real life, with less suffering and greater joy. I am not using as a measure of superiority the common notion that everything that comes later is better than what was there before (we tend to think like this when we hear words like "evolution" and "progress"). The measure is quality of life: those who lead happier, calmer, better lives are more mature. More mature individuals overcome turbulence and adversities faster. They can also be considered stronger, since they are able to tolerate greater and even more drawn out suffering. They are able to move on, feeling less hurt and traumatized, which always ensures a happier future.

Flávio Gikovate

1

The issue of the forming and development of human reason remains obscure and poorly resolved. I like to make a comparison with computers, machines with which we are growing increasingly familiar. It is as if we were born with the hardware almost completely formed, but completely devoid of software. The hardware is directly related to everything biological, including our genetic equipment. The software, however, is one of the most important acquisitions of our species, which was probably ready to develop it for more than one hundred thousand years, but only managed to start the process in the last ten thousand years with the acquisition of language, which was indispensable to the use of our biological potential. Our privileged biology only became effective, therefore, through a process of socialization and cultural acquisition.

The first stages in the forming of what we call human reason take place in the first few months and years of life, when children begin to recognize the words that name the objects around them, and later those that define movements, actions, and qualities. In this manner, the conditions are created for the building of more and more complex phrases, and psychological processes become increasingly sophisticated, capable of more intricate, subtle operations. At some stage two of the most important human acquisitions appear: the ability to build sentences, which means that a child can have his or her own points of view; and, going a step further, the ability to develop thoughts that involve hypotheses, in other words, situations that are not actually being lived. An extraordinarily complex psychological process with unlimited possibilities — our ability to imagine things that don't exist — is thus created. The ability to make suppositions and consider possibilities offers our species unusual, unique perspectives. It underpins our ability to put ourselves in other's shoes and develop a real moral sentiment. It is also directly related to our creative capacity, which is as essential in the sciences as in the arts.

Further to my observation about children's ability to develop their own points of view, I believe we should consider another important element in their makeup: the children themselves! That is, in addition to the social world, parents, media, and traumatic experiences that happen to everyone at some stage, we must also consider the way in which a child has registered, reflected on, and interpreted each fact of his or her life. Even identical twins, who have identical biology and have been brought up in the same social and family context, can think and act very differently to one another as a result of the particular way in which they understood what happened to them in their childhood.

The subject of the constitution and sophistication of reason is extremely complex and it may take us years to get a better grasp on it. To say we are making great advances and will soon have the basic answers as to how the brain produces thought is naïve — or deliberately misleading.

three

The first value judgment I am trying to establish has to do with quality of life — not a pre-established notion of what is good or bad. **Those who are more controlled, more skilled at dealing with intense emotional situations — involving anger, jealousy, envy, etc. — are stronger. Those who have a "short fuse" and explode more easily for less important reasons are weaker.** Those who are able to put themselves in others' shoes and comprehend their suffering are stronger, while navel-gazers, who only see the world from their own point of view, are weaker. People who devote themselves more to others are stronger, and those who are more concerned with looking after themselves are weaker.

We usually treat weaker people with kid gloves because we know they react badly in situations of pain or adversity. Curiously, these people are often seen as more sensitive, which is why we tend to spare them certain things. This confusion runs deep, since many people believe that individuals with "shorts fuses" have "strong personalities", which suggests they are actually stronger than others. Because this confusion in the use of terms generally works in their favour, we are better off dealing with this subject with more objectivity and less word play. Weaker individuals, who can generically be considered selfish, are those who are more concerned with themselves than others, and need to receive more than they give. In my opinion, this shows an obvious deficit in their inner economy.

People with higher tolerance of obstacles and psychological pain often develop a curious behaviour pattern that can be referred to as generosity. It seems they are not content with merely being stronger and, thus, self-sufficient. Everything would lead us to believe that they desperately need to devote themselves to more selfish sorts. Generosity implies giving more than receiving, an obvious sign of a surplus in their inner economy.

What is most interesting about generosity is its non-obligatory nature. While the selfish have to seek externally whatever they lack because they are unable to generate everything they need internally, the generous could easily not be like this: all they'd have to do is keep for themselves everything they generate — or generate less. But this isn't what happens. The generous feel a kind of compulsion to give. It strikes me as logical that they should direct such dedication at those who not only need it but demand it emphatically; that is, the selfish.

One of the most stable, constant dualities, typical of intimate human relationships, is thus composed. Most couples are like this, as are many societal ties, relationships between friends and between parents and children. Stronger, more self-sufficient individuals seem to have an uncontrollable desire to exert their strength on weaker individuals. They lose much of their self-sufficiency as a result of this desire. The generous seem to love giving to others, and can only do so to the selfish, since other generous sorts also want to give.

When the generous receive something (and this can be a simple birthday present), they feel somewhat diminished, humiliated even. A closer look at this simple fact, which is easy to find and observe, may help explain this kind of behaviour. Generosity is typical of those who are superior and is designed to humiliate those who receive, that is, the selfish. In order for our reason to warp in such a way, it must be under the influence of a very strong feeling. I believe it is time to introduce it.

Vanity[2] is the part of our sexual instinct that feeds on feeling strong, when we distinguish ourselves in some way, or awaken the attention and admiration of other people. Vanity is characterized by an intense feeling of sexual arousal. It is fuelled by the act of giving, exercising generosity. A person's vanity is insulted when they feel like the underdog, that is, when they receive. This insult, in turn, gives rise to a feeling of humiliation. The generous thus puff up with vanity while the selfish are humiliated.

---

[2] The term vanity, present in biblical texts — very emphatically so in Ecclesiastes — and the reflections of most great thinkers up until the 19th century, disappeared from the scene in the context of psychoanalysis. It was replaced, in a way that I consider dangerous, with the term narcissism, which I have spoken out against on many occasions because I believe it obscures more about our subjectivity than it clarifies. Vanity is a fundamental part of autoerotic phenomena, present from very early on in

▸

our lives, but which gains great vitality with puberty. Since sex and love are not differentiated from one another in the radical way I believe essential in psychoanalysis, narcissism, which should mean "love for oneself", is used to refer to the presence of an important erotic ingredient related to the vague excitement we feel when we get other people's attention, whether or not for sexual reasons. I believe the most appropriate term to be the traditional one (vanity), since narcissism is also associated to a degree with histrionic behaviours (such as gross self-promotion), extroversion, selfishness, and so many other characteristics that are neither universal nor obligatory. Vanity, however, being part of our sexual instinct, is in everyone, including the more discreet, who pride themselves on their simplicity and frugal lifestyles.

A more complete reflection on two essential aspects of vanity is called for: firstly, that the pleasure of showing off and getting other people's attention implies absolute dependence on the outside world and, secondly, that the desire to stand out from the crowd is enormous, and requires a search for more unusual qualities that will attract looks of admiration and even desire. This is not the place for such an in-depth analysis, but I would like to emphasize that the intense desire for distinction inherent in this aspect of our sexuality can seriously warp the way we think and live. We become more dependent than we should on public opinion and, consequently, lose in terms of freedom and creativity. We go to exhausting lengths to acquire special skills or positions that do not necessarily bring us any closer to happiness. Not to mention the fact that — due to the intense and ephemeral nature of the pleasure of new distinction — we tend to seek continuous and ever-growing repetition, characteristic of all addictions.

four

With the inception of this pleasure in giving, reinforced by vanity and the humiliation to which the selfish must necessarily submit themselves, it is easy to understand how they start to envy[3] the generous. It causes people to lash out as a reaction to humiliation, since the act of receiving is seen as a weakness, a sign that one is the underdog. The selfish thus react to the "dedication" of the generous with violence and ungratefulness. It's not surprising, considering that they interpret the donation they have received as an aggression that humiliated them. I am not conviced that aggressive actions are typical of our species. I think, most of the time, that what exists are reactions, although they are often responses to veiled actions or even to situations incorrectly interpreted as such. I am excluding from this analysis situations of extreme adversity, in which a person might act in an aggressive or even brutal manner in order to survive.

If the generous act compulsively and intentionally, that is, if they want to humiliate the selfish, then the obvious conclusion is that this is also a reaction. So the generous also envy the selfish. Herein lies another complex and controversial problem. It appears to be a given that envy exists. What's more, envy, like love, is born of admiration. If the generous are emotionally attracted to the selfish, it is because they admire them. They admire qualities they do not possess, such that envy manifests together with love. **Now what? In what ways do the generous feel so inferior to the selfish that they must envy them? Aren't the selfish supposed to be the weaker ones? How can the strong envy the weak?**

People who develop a higher frustration tolerance are those who also manage to put themselves in other people's shoes and, when they imagine their suffering, they deal with this indirect pain without renouncing the process. They learn, in so doing, to respect the rights of others. This is because other people's suffering as victims of injustice makes them suffer vicariously. They develop a true moral sentiment, a concern for the rights of others, a conviction that others have equal rights to themselves. When they discover they have caused others to suffer, they feel an enormous sadness, an emotion we like to call guilt.

We know that the selfish interrupt this process of putting themselves in other people's shoes precisely because of the pain involved. They are not concerned about the rights of others because injustices suffered by other people do not cause them any pain. They don't develop a true moral sentiment, which resides inside us, reining us in, and limiting us. Their limits are only determined by external circumstances and fear of reprisal. The selfish don't feel guilt[4]. (This doesn't mean that they don't use the word or claim to regret things. Uttering a word, however, is very different to feeling its meaning.) The selfish don't possess the internal braking mechanism that limits the actions of the generous.

The selfish ask for, demand, and claim for themselves, in every possible way, attention and favours. When they do so emphatically they realize just how much it moves the generous. When the generous recognize suffering in the selfish, they start to feel guilty — without call. They will be accused of being the cause of that pain if they don't pander to the desires of the selfish. If they are unable to resist, they will give in and do things they really don't want to do. It's as if the generous were slaves to their feelings of guilt and therefore defenceless, even when the claims of the selfish strike them as absurd and uncalled for. It is true that the generous feel strong and, consequently, love to give. But because they are incapable of defending themselves from what we call "emotional blackmail" (and the selfish know it), they start to feel exploited, used, and abused.

These feelings of guilt make it hard for the generous to tolerate the suffering — real or imagined — of "others". This leads to successive concessions that they and others interpret as weakness. They give in because they are unable to resist external pressure, whether in the form of intimidation or situations that inspire guilt. At first the selfish make their demands using the resources of intimidation. If their threats do not get the desired results, they then move on to emotional blackmail, a condition in which they start to show great suffering — and even desperation. When the generous give in because they can't resist the pressure, they experience it in a very different way to the pleasure of giving, which feeds their vanity and makes them feel superior. Now they feel weak, abused, robbed. Unable to act any other way, they cede, and start feeling resentment and anger toward the selfish — as well as the obvious feeling of humiliation, a consequence of having been pressured into doing something against their will.

It is important to note that anger doesn't bring about a behavioural change that makes the generous less vulnerable. On the contrary, it reinforces the generous attitude, now completely unconnected to the desire to be useful and the pleasure of giving to others. The intention is now to humiliate or avenge oneself of humiliation. The selfish, in turn, feel increasingly envious of the strength and inner wealth of the generous. Humiliated, they demand more and more, which leads the generous to give in a manner increasingly associated with hostile, aggressive feelings. And so on.

In this context, both the generous and the selfish feel violated and are forced to recognize that their opponents possess powerful weapons. The generous, because of their inability to deal effectively with the elements underpinning their feelings of guilt, develop a true weakness to the selfish. They consequentially lose their condition of superiority and are therefore perfectly capable of envying them.

3

Envy is a complex emotion, because it is an aggressive reaction that arises from the way we deal with certain differences that make us feel at a disadvantage. We insist on hierarchizing the differences we perceive. We admire people who have qualities we would like to have. We admire, but do not take joy in, differences that are unfavourable to us. On the contrary, we feel offended and humiliated, and our vanity — which we sometimes prefer to call pride — is wounded. We start feeling hostility, as if the person with the admirable quality were an attacker, someone who hurts us simply because they have something we would like to have. We feel violated and lash out. We are the only ones who recognize the aggressive act, since the person with the quality we admire but do not possess hasn't done anything to us — at least not overtly. We react to an aggression detected and decoded as such by our way of thinking.

Many people interpret aggressive manifestations of envy as actions rather than reactions. This is because it doesn't enter into their minds that we may be reading a subtle form of aggression into the behaviour of someone we admire. The object of our envy doesn't always intend to hurt us with their superiority. But they do anyway. For example, when a wealthy person lends money to a poor relative, their actions will end up provoking envious hostility in the one receiving. The receiver feels humiliated, the underdog, diminished by the fact of needing help — and wishes they were in the position of the wealthy relative. The subtlest form of envy is simply the desire to be in the position of the one who is admired. When this isn't possible, a desire to bring the admired one down to the receiver's own condition can surface — when possible, in reality, and when not possible, in destructive fantasies. At any rate, whenever someone lends money to a friend who cannot return it, they will lose the money and the friend.

My clinical experience has taught me that there are a few people who don't feel envy. They are able to admire and value the achievements of someone close to them, and are truly happy to be around those who have enjoyed some kind of success. Unfortunately, they are rare exceptions. At any rate, I would also like to emphasize that admiration is the basis for another important emotion: love. Admiration has two offspring: love and envy. It's no accident that these two emotions are so often simultaneously directed at a single object.

4

I think some observations are in order about the differences between feelings and emotions, terms we use as synonyms. Some authors use the term "feeling" to describe things we experience directly, such as pain, fear, aggression, and sexual desire. They speak of emotions when the processes are more complex, when there is some kind of intervention of reason. Here would be adult love and the jealousy that usually accompanies it, envy, and also guilt. In all of these situations, our reason participates in choice making, as is the case with love and jealousy; establishing hierarchies, as is the case with envy; or trying to imagine another person's suffering, as is the case with guilt.

I am adamant in my view that guilt depends on our ability for reason having reached a particular degree of sophistication, which makes it possible for us to try to put ourselves in someone else's shoes and imagine their suffering due to something we have done to them — a fairly subtle psychological operation. As such, I don't see how one can consider guilt to participate in the subjectivity of a child of 1, 2 or even 3 years of age. The sadness derived from feeling that we have caused unnecessary pain in others, which is responsible for our internal braking mechanism (since causing pain occasions a pain that is perhaps greater than the one we have caused), requires fairly sophisticated reasoning. Moreover, it requires that the process of putting oneself in another's shoes is not interrupted because of the difficulty many children have dealing with suffering and psychological pain.

It seems clear that guilt is one of the emotions that most requires the interference of reason, since it has little, if any, basis in primitive feelings. Adult love is based on the primitive feeling that unites children to their mothers. Envy is related to wounded vanity, which in turn is a natural component of our sexual instinct. Guilt depends essentially on psychological operations and the ability to identify with another human being's suffering, which implies the development of an adequate amount of inner strength. It is not surprising, therefore, that it is absent in such a large number of people.

I do not feel that I have finished exploring the issue of guilt, just as I am more and more convinced that it is an emotion without an innate, biological basis. Perhaps it is related to pain, through the process of identification established when we put ourselves in someone else's shoes. Perhaps it has to do with fear when it arises because of the violation of some absolute ethical principle based on religious doctrine, a controversial topic that I do not intend to explore in this book. One example may clarify this: when teenagers masturbate and feel guilty for having acted out of keeping with their religious convictions, they may feel fear of divine reprisal, above

▶

all. Even so, it is an extremely complex issue, always dependent on multiple psychological operations.

If it is true that guilt does not have a biological basis, it is easy to understand that the number of people who have this inner braking mechanism varies enormously from era to era and culture to culture. In today's world, in which there is greater permissiveness and people are freer to act on their desires (especially of a sexual nature), it is quite possible that we are living in an era in which guilt is felt by considerably fewer people than a century ago, when religious precepts were much stricter, more rigid, and more influential.

five

It is fairly evident that the giving behaviour of the generous loses its purity as time goes by. While in the beginning it received the important reinforcement of vanity (which can no longer be considered such a pure ally), it is now strengthened by resentment and anger, feelings that arise when the generous feel exploited. Additionally, they come to envy the selfish, who, because of their inability to feel guilt, are much freer to enjoy life's pleasures more intensely, especially those of an erotic nature. Here is an example to clarify what I am talking about: selfish men usually find it easier to approach women, acting directly to seduce them and get them into bed. Since they don't worry about any suffering they may inflict by virtue of the fact that they are only looking for casual physical intimacy, they act with a brazenness that is impossible for the generous, who are always worried about hurting others' feelings. So, what happens? The generous feel frustrated and incompetent, as they also wish for relaxed, casual contact, and end up envying the freedom the selfish are able to enjoy due to their lack of guilt. This envy can be so intense that it overrides moral reflection, which would otherwise lead the generous to criticize the disloyal conduct of the selfish.

Because of all the things that reinforce generosity, individuals feel increasingly locked into their mode of behaviour, as if they were totally "addicted" to it, in addition to the fact that it is the very behaviour expected of them. They get used to the idea that they are loved because they are like this, and start to fear that their refusal to keep acting in the same way, always serving everyone else, will mean immediate rejection and abandonment. They convince themselves that they are only accepted because of the "something extra" they always manage to give. This helps create a sense of inferiority; a feeling that, if they show what they really feel, they won't be as readily accepted.

This feeling of inferiority is made worse by self-criticism, because they recognize that they are afraid, incapable of hurting those who offend them. They end up not being able to defend themselves from any kind of attack, no matter how uncalled for. This is because they are unable to hurt someone else under any circumstance, since it would occasion a strong feeling of guilt, causing them great personal pain. They can't hurt anyone, not even when it means saying no to the whims of the selfish. The selfish will interpret their refusal to serve them as selfishness. That is: not giving into a selfish person's unfair demands will be seen as selfishness! **The generous feel slave to their dedication as much for inner reasons as for fear of what others will think.**

Their generous conduct thus tends to remain a vice that is very difficult to shake. It does enormous harm to the individual, but it seems that the little self-esteem they have left is derived from their exploitation and inability to say no to it under any circumstance. Anger, resentment and a thirst for revenge must exist, even if hidden away in the basement of the subconscious, which is where we send the emotions and feelings we don't like to feel. This revenge strikes in the form of reinforced generous conduct, which, at this stage in the process, should have undergone a name change.

Thus, generosity, which in itself isn't obligatory and could quite easily be demonstrated sporadically, becomes a constant behaviour pattern, which the generous themselves see as a sub product of personal weaknesses: fear and guilt. This fear is a peculiar fear, different to that which we all feel. It is the fear of striking out, not just of being struck. It is the fear of making someone else suffer, even in the form of a reaction to an aggression that came from them. It is thus a kind of "obligatory kindness", which means it is no longer a manifestation of strength and self-sufficiency. It has become a new kind of dependence. While the selfish depend in a direct, practical manner, the generous become dependent because they are unable to take a strong stance with others, especially the selfish. Their symbiosis becomes more and more obligatory due to their reciprocal admiration and modes of behaviour. Their intimacy, however, will always be tormented by feelings such as anger, envy, reciprocal humiliation, and a reciprocal desire to retaliate. It is a battle from which neither can flee, since no one wants to lose, and it becomes an unpleasant, ongoing struggle.

Neither one can escape this fight, in which there are no winners. It is a game of tit for tat. The act of undue giving is at once a strike and retaliation: the more the generous give, the more they also feel exploited, and further humiliate the selfish, who feel victorious as their increasingly ludicrous demands are met, at the same time that they feel increasingly humiliated by the proof of their opponent's inner wealth. Considering that most couples live like this, there is no doubt left that the phenomenon we refer to as love needs profound reassessment.

 six

One of the greatest hindrances in the study of psychological processes is probably the risk of trying to understand the behaviour of those with whom we can't identify for lack of similar subjective experiences. For men, for example, it is extraordinarily difficult to understand how the female mind works. And vice-versa. For the generous, the selfish are strange creatures, and it is very hard to try to decode them using themselves as a basis for comparison. Perhaps not even Freud, an excellent observer of the human psyche, was able to fully understand this matter. He believed, based on appearance, that selfishness was related to narcissism and that narcissists were those who loved themselves to such a point that they were unable to love anyone else. But the facts tell quite a different story. Narcissists not only love themselves, but they also have no other interest beyond being loved, a condition in which demanding and receiving more than they deserve comes more easily.

I too might be mistaken in my observations. Nevertheless, I think that after almost forty years of work I have a duty to present my conclusions. **I think that at some stage in life the selfish become aware that the generous**

envy them (in the same way that they also envy the generous). The generous envy the lack of inner brakes that frees the selfish to lie and deceive others. They envy the ease with which they enjoy material objects that often weren't obtained with the sweat off their own backs — the generous tend to have reservations about this, perhaps for fear of deliberately provoking the envy of others, which ultimately means they themselves will suffer. The selfish, on the other hand, love to be the centre of attention and incite envy in others. They exercise their vanity shamelessly. **When they realize that the generous envy them, they go out of their way to appear extraordinarily happy and at peace with themselves — which they suppose, and not without reason, is how the generous see them.** They try to look pleased with themselves, like the winners of the fight they know hasn't been and never will be won, since they are perfectly aware of their vital dependence on the generous.

Posing as cheerful, outgoing, sensual and happy, they may actually manage to convince quite a few people that they are all of these things. I think it's a big act, theatrics. This isn't the real idea the selfish have of themselves (at least not the only one); they know all too well they are bluffing. In fact, if the selfish don't have a set of inner, interiorized moral brakes, I don't know what to make, in their case, of the traditional psychoanalytical idea of the subconscious. I imagine that, in order for a feeling or emotion to spring from the conscious, the inner moral instance that gives rise to it must first exist![5]

The selfish try to pass themselves off as strong, but they know they are weak, fly off the handle when they run into obstacles, and are dependent on the devotion of the generous, on whom they are shameless — though humiliated — parasites. They are impulsive because they have little determination and discipline, not because they are strong and fearless. (The selfish are fearful in precisely the same proportion as the generous; what they don't have is the fear of hurting others.) They have a great capacity for simulation, since they are not committed to the truth or a code of inner values. They pose as good-natured, strong and happy, although this isn't how they feel on the inside. They are not concerned with coherence or intellectual rigor. They are completely different to the generous, who, turning a blind eye to their obvious differences, bend over backwards to try to understand them using themselves as a basis for comparison, which can lead to serious misconceptions. They all use the same vocabulary: they say that they love, feel guilt and don't lie, etc. They use the same words, but don't experience similar emotions. This danger of misunderstanding is present whenever different people use the same words. For example: when women say, "so-and-so is hot," are they feeling exactly the same thing men feel when they express themselves in this way?

5

My clinical experience has led me to progressively revise the traditional positions of dynamic psychology that so influenced me early in my career. I am more and more convinced that the number of people who don't feel guilt is greater than traditionally thought. It used to be said that only people with clearly anti-social behaviour were devoid of guilt. I see the lack of this emotion, however, in all more selfish individuals, not just the extreme cases. I haven't been able to identify signs of behaviour based on unconscious processes in those who don't feel guilt, since their manipulative attitudes are absolutely intentional and deliberate. They act on impulse, it is true, but always for their own benefit. They occasionally regret actions that have been poorly thought through, but only when such actions lead to unexpected, inconvenient developments. As such, their regret is strictly operational and doesn't contain the sadness born of having caused others undue suffering — which wouldn't bother them in the slightest if it wasn't accompanied by negative consequences for themselves.

Even in more generous individuals, who undeniably feel guilt, unconscious mechanisms strike me as increasingly uncommon. The permissive nature of society, the liberating influence of psychoanalysis itself, and the way it has made us think about our condition have helped people to be a lot more honest with themselves and accept all of their feelings more easily. Almost everyone believes they have the right to feel envy, to wish for the death of those who hurt them (perhaps with the exception of some cases involving close relatives) and to covet "thy neighbour's wife". The impression I have is that the generous still have inner moral brakes, which stop them from acting in keeping with what they feel. They learn that thoughts are free, but action must still be mediated by reflection on the rights of others. More selfish types tend to try to concretize everything they think, especially in the realm of desire, because they don't cope well with being up against limits.

I sometimes think the discovery of the subconscious was a very precise blow from the founder of psychoanalysis that marked the beginning of the end of this psychological instance. This is because, by describing the peculiarities and content of the subconscious, he made us aware of processes hitherto unknown to us. In one fell swoop he discovered the subconscious and made it disappear.

7

seven

It appears undeniable that the generous see the selfish as they present themselves, which means their act is a big success. The generous admire and value the boldness born of their lack of moral sentiment, which is curious for many reasons, not least the fact that the lack of inner brakes on the part of the selfish means it is no great feat to act "against" the generous. The generous admire the ease with which the selfish enjoy material pleasures, which, for the generous, are prohibited or limited to small daily quotas. Their limitations make them feel inferior, but they also know that the selfish need them for everything and, in this aspect, feel superior. Their feelings are a double-edged sword that can give rise to enchantment, envy and anger on the one hand, and contempt and the desire to humiliate on the other. Deep down the selfish feel the same way toward the generous. Neither of these two very different groups is able to define itself clearly in relation to its opposite. They are unable to establish a hierarchy between themselves. Additionally, the mixed feelings they have for one another cause them to strike out with violence, each using the weapons available to them.

We thus live in a world in which people exhibit two different modes of behaviour. Such a polarized world

also dominates, obviously, more intimate human relationships. It leaks into all aspects of social life and is transmitted from one generation to the next by example. This polarity crystallizes around essential conceptions that impregnate everyone to a degree: we accept the two divine principles of gods and demons, and the values that, through the centuries, we have come to refer to as "good" and "evil".

eight

At this point, I would like to make some observations about child raising. **Children grow up in homes where, as a rule, one of the parents is generous and the other, selfish (I don't think there is any distinction between the number of men and women who are generous or selfish, such that the generous one could be either the father or the mother).** Each child is exposed, therefore, to both personality types — right from start. From the point of view of a small child, there doesn't seem to be any hierarchical difference between the parents' personality types: both appear equally valid. This is because the parents are together, and also because the children witness moments of tenderness between them (as well as fights, which may also be frequent), which suggests reciprocal admiration — the precursor of romantic love. **The first child of a couple characterized by this polarity will be free to "choose" the parent with whom they identify and whose footsteps they will try to follow.**

Obviously, when I use the word "choose" I do not mean that a child does so by using his or her fledgling reason. This is not about children understanding that there are two kinds of human beings as far as values are concerned. They are able to perceive, from very early on, that there are two kinds of anatomy, defining the two sexes. But in this case the differences are visible to the naked eye! No child looks from father to mother, assesses the peculiarities of each and decides to identify with the personality type of one. It is all much more intuitive and depends on countless other variables that I won't go into here. The fact is that each child will tend to adhere to one of these two groups; that is, they won't be capable of "creating" their own personality type, different to the ones they observe. This "choice" depends on the innate peculiarities of each child, their sex and the type (generous or selfish) of the parent of the same sex, with whom the child establishes a more consistent emotional bond and with whom they feel more protected and secure. Social norms also interfere in the way children turn out, since they can determine the importance placed on characteristics such as extroversion, success at all costs, the values taught at the religious centres that the family attends, and so on.

It is interesting to note that the child is accepted in any case, no matter what their choice. They will be seen as having "taken after" their mother or father, or "Uncle So-and-So". Everything is treated as if we were faced with a "genetic" fatalism that determines and validates both personality types. The truly curious thing happens with the second child: they will be the opposite of the first! They will always "take after" the other side. It is more than evident that we are looking at a determinant stronger than

genetics or mere coincidence. We are looking at one of the first manifestations of the inevitable sibling rivalry, their dispute for the love and attention of their parents, who, unfortunately, have to be shared. The second child, being the opposite of the first, occupies the vacant space in the constellation of that particular family, and thus finds their nucleus of attention and gratification. The third child is "freer" than the second, because once again they are able to choose between the two types. This is the most common family structure, in which there are the two sides, in both generations. The original models are reproduced: selfish and generous.

A more in-depth analysis shows that the greatest aim of the best educators, to instil an inner moral sentiment in all children (who, in virtue of this, will be respectful, disciplined and dedicated in their studies and chores), stands in direct opposition to the facts, in other words, it is an obvious impossibility. **There is no school environment capable of outweighing what happens at home. By the time they get there, children are already one type or another and tend to behave at school as they do at home. The more selfish ones are more disruptive, while the more generous ones are better behaved and try harder.** The observable facts obviously start to depend on a number of new ingredients (which are not the focus of this book but which should be mentioned), such as intelligence and special aptitudes. Children who are selfish, but very intelligent and talented, may be outstanding students in spite of their irreverence. When they get attention for their good results, they may develop a taste for study and perform very well. In the same manner, children who are generous and less talented may lose interest in their studies and not take pleasure in the acquisition of knowledge.

nine

Generally speaking, from the point of view of moral development and emotional maturity, schools are still dependent on what happens to children in the family context and any changes that take place there. Official discourse is currently showing signs that people are becoming aware of the need for change in how they choose spouses. **Until just a few decades ago, it was said that "opposites attract",** as if this were part of an inexorable fatality (like magnets, objects with which we have little in common), **but now people talk about "soul mates". Unfortunately, and for complex reasons, this new notion has yet to show real signs that it is leaving the realm of words** and bringing change in the actions of young people.

Among the complicated reasons why this new notion isn't becoming fact more quickly (although it will be extremely welcome when it does), **I first cite the most obvious: in order to seek a romantic partner similar to ourselves, they would have to be the object of our admiration. For this to happen we would have to improve our self-image, such that we would stop being attracted to those who are our opposites. In other words, we would have to be able to undo the whole "diabolical story" I have just described.**

A second reason has to do with the actual viability of relationships between similar people. A relationship between generous people is much more feasible than a relationship between selfish people. The generous are more tolerant, calmer, and we can imagine them living in harmony — that is, of course, if they are able to learn to receive more, even if only a little. The selfish, who are more impulsive and likely to fly off the handle when faced with obstacles, would tend to live in a state of constant friction. I also think they are able to read one another much better than the generous do (in other words, the selfish are probably able to fool the generous better than they can others of their kind). They know they are not really at peace with themselves and know that this is probably also true of their partners, which radically affects their ability to admire them. Additionally, trust — so necessary in romantic involvement, since it is what attenuates our fear of suffering as a result of disloyalty and abandonment — will also be somewhat shaky. This is due to the lack of emotional control of those who are more intolerant and incapable of accepting a series of frustrations. Moreover, it is hard to imagine the selfish really managing to accept themselves to the extent that they can truly be attracted to their "soul mate".

A third reason, which will be my focus at other moments in this book, has to do with the fear we all feel of happiness[6]. When we get very close to what we believe to be a state of plenitude, in which we lack for nothing (and successful love is one situation in which we feel this), a vague fear creeps up on us and we feel as if risk and danger are just around the corner. It's as if a great tragedy has started prowling around us and will catch up with us at any moment. Our state of panic and terror can be so great that we are unable to see any other alternative but to destroy that which "provokes" our happiness as well as our fear. If a very intense romantic connection is at the root of this happiness, as happens when like-minded people come together, what usually happens is that they will find a range of external reasons, of relative value, to justify the decision to "cut themselves free" from the relationship. As a result, the overwhelming majority of intense love affairs end with the separation of the lovers[7].

I can cite, even if only briefly, a forth motive, related to our sexuality. A curious and unexpected fact is that relationships between generous people — the most common kind of connection based on affinities — is usually accompanied by sexual difficulties, especially for men. Completely different processes take place in relationships between opposites, where sexuality is part of the power play and the silent war between them.

It seems that in relationships founded on harmony we lack some of the ingredients that are an essential part of our sexual experiences. There will be no doubt as to the fidelity of the other, which takes the wind out of the sails of the game of seduce-and-conquer that so stimulates our eroticism. The most profound and complex ingredients of this story have to do with the dramatic association between sex and aggressiveness, a registered trademark of so many cultures, perhaps an unexpected sub product of the chronic war between "good" and "evil". In other words, erotic elements have always been related to reciprocal envy and are part of the processes of humiliation inherent to that which we, inappropriately, call loving relationships[8].

6

I described the mechanism of the fear of happiness in 1980, and I am becoming more and more aware of the fundamental role it plays in our psychological processes, in spite of the fact that it is neglected by most people, specialists or not. I believe that fear of happiness has been at the root of superstitious thinking since the beginning of time. It is, therefore, essentially biological in nature, and accompanies us in proportions that can vary from person to person. When someone asks us how we are and we say we are fine, we often perform some kind of ritual (such as knocking on wood) to protect ourselves from the "wrath of the gods" or the envy of others. Certain numbers are considered dangerous — to this day, many buildings in New York (one of the most forward-looking cities in the world) do not have a thirteenth floor!

This is a fairly complex phenomenon that in most cases only manifests clearly after puberty. My theory is that it is a universal traumatic experience (the trauma of birth), activated by ingredients perhaps related to vanity and other prior psychological processes. (It is not uncommon in the case of phobias for a particular traumatic experience, dormant for years, to suddenly resurface as a result of a new event somehow related to it.) I think it works something like this: there we were in the womb, where our brain was formed, in an almost homeostatic condition. Everything was more or less in order. This is perhaps our first psychological imprint, which is evidently non-verbal and, for this reason, difficult to erase. The following imprint is the dramatic disruption of this equilibrium: the hour of our birth. In other words, being born is a transition from harmony to disharmony. We were in paradise and then we were kicked out. We are thus always seeking to return to our original condition of peace and harmony — although, after our psychological processes have been activated, we come to see this condition as extremely tedious. The closer we get to this ideal, which is particularly strong when we feel loved and accepted by the person who is the object of our love, we first feel plenitude, followed by the fear that it may be once again disrupted by a dramatic experience — now perhaps through our own death or the death of someone very special. Faced with such a possibility, it makes sense that we tend to avoid or even destroy the paradisiacal condition we wanted so badly.

7

This isn't the place for an exhaustive analysis of the phenomenon of love, a topic I have explored in two of my most important works: *Uma nova visão do amor* (*A New Vision of Love*) and *Ensaios sobre o amor e a solidão* (*Essays on Love and Solitude*). I would just like to state once again that passion appears to be composed of two ingredients: a very intense feeling of love, due to the lovers' great affinities, and very intense fear, derived precisely from the plenitude and happiness that accompanies this romantic connection. The fact is that in the overwhelming majority of cases fear predominates and gives rise to a strong self-destructive streak, which seeks arguments to justify the separation of the loving couple. It is a shame, because, if they had the courage to keep the relationship going in spite of their fear, they'd see that little by little it tends to wane — something often confused with a waning of romantic intensity, which gets in the way of an adequate assessment of the subjective facts.

I believe, therefore, that there are strong self-destructive mechanisms in our subjectivity. I don't attribute them to a so-called "death instinct", which is the way psychoanalysts interpret the same phenomenon. I believe it has to do with our fear of happiness, which is strictly related to birth, not death. We desire and fear the return of our "paradise lost". I don't see how we can wish for death, which is something we have not experienced. We tend to be more destructive precisely when we are very close to happiness. Knowing this should give us the means to at least limit these destructive tendencies (even if we can't completely eradicate them), because when we become aware of the mechanism, we can carefully position ourselves when good things happen to us.

8

Difficulty associating sex and love is more intense, frequent and visible in generous men. This is somewhat obvious, since the selfish are busier worrying about being loved than loving. Additionally, since they are less critical of cultural norms that disqualify women, they don't make any great effort to distinguish between them. They are all "women" and, therefore, to be seen and treated with disregard. Generous men tend to look up to and respect the women to whom they are emotionally attracted, such that they feel smaller than them. In these conditions they have great difficulty becoming aroused. Since the same thing is not necessarily true of generous women, they have a hard time understanding what's going on (it is difficult to understand what we don't feel), and they attribute such difficulties to flaws in themselves or think the men are lying when they say they love them.

This only illustrates one of the many difficulties that people in good-quality loving relationships have to go through until they manage to work things out sexually.

Because of the fear of happiness, if their sexual experiences are very gratifying and considerably increase their quota of happiness, they will be paradoxically infrequent: the sex is great and only happens every once in a while, precisely because the people involved can't bear more than a certain amount of happiness.

Couples who are always fighting don't have these problems! They are not afraid of happiness because they are not close to it. As a result, they often have a richer sex life than those who live in harmony. Additionally, as I wrote in my book *A liberta-ção sexual* (*Sexual Liberation*), which deals extensively with the subject, fights fuel the anger and insecurities that so stimulate eroticism in almost all of us, who were brought up in this obviously pathological social context.

10. ten

The more I think and reflect on all of these issues, which I have been doing on a daily basis for some thirty years, the more convinced I am of the importance and revolutionary potential in the construction of good-quality loving bonds. I believe such bonds to be the point of departure for any real and consistent social advancement. I think this not just because marriages and families are still the environment in which the main characteristics of future generations are forged, but also because I believe that it is within the most intimate relationships that the best conditions are created for overcoming (and, unfortunately, perpetuating) this dramatic war between "good" and "evil".

11

eleven

Before I go on, I would like to make a complementary observation about my way of seeing and classifying people, which may seem a little radical at first — and which, in a way, only reproduces the duality that has accompanied us throughout the millenniums through religious speculation about good and bad divinities. In both selfishness and generosity there are individual specifics masked by the generalizations I'm obliged to make here. Moreover, it is a way of assessing people that implies a scale. That is, there are people who are more and less generous, those who are closer or farther from the point of equilibrium located on the frontier between selfishness and generosity. The same thing happens with the selfish, such that there are those who are not terribly far from this point of equilibrium and those who are at the outer extreme of the scale; that is, delinquents, who are devoid of guilt and don't respect social norms because they don't fear reprisal — which reins in the actions of the selfish who are closer to this point of equilibrium. The generous, in addition to their inner brakes, also feel limited by this external mechanism.

Delinquents — people who are fearless and totally unscrupulous — win the admiration of other transgressors who are far from the point of equilibrium but who still have a certain braking mechanism fed by fear. Transgressors who feel fear look up to and allow themselves to be led by those who are completely fearless. They don't admire the generous at all, which is a rather odd and complete inversion of values that only manifests at the extreme end of the scale, in the outer reaches of selfishness. This is, however, a dramatic manifestation of a personality disorder, which leads to entirely anti-social behaviour and, fortunately, corresponds to a very small percentage of the population — perhaps somewhere between 0.5% and 1% of the total. This percentage is not significant enough for me to address in this work, which deals with the psychology of people referred to as "normal" because they are part of the majority.

At the outer extreme of the scale of generosity are the saints, "good" in the purest sense, for whom the act of giving isn't contaminated by any kind of human motivation. Although I find it hard to believe that there are individuals completely devoid of vanity, I do think it is possible for many of us to have moments of pure solidarity and altruism. **I believe it is important to distinguish between altruism and generosity[9]. Altruism is an impersonal act of giving and dedication. Different to what happens with generosity, where the giving is to specific, intimate individuals (spouses, children, employees), altruism is exercised more generally and, as a rule, is shrouded in anonymity.** Situations also arise in which we can identify with causes that don't affect us (they neither benefit nor harm us), and we can devote ourselves to them selflessly, at least in essential aspects. The most tangible example of this is the mobilization that takes place, even from a distance, when humanitarian support must be found for a group of people annihilated by misery, whether through starvation, natural tragedy, or epidemic disease. **I believe this to be the essence of human solidarity, which derives from the evolution of our capacity for reason and has no parallel among other animals. I think this is one point of departure for us to finally understand our species as unique, very different to all others, in spite of any genetic similarities.**

9

We are capable of putting ourselves in other people's shoes and imagining what they might be feeling. When they feel pain (at least what we are able to perceive based on what we see), we feel the pain we think they are feeling. As we know, the selfish interrupt this process because they don't deal well with pain. We can feel the pain of people with whom we have no contact whatsoever as well as of those who are dear to us. The phenomenon of altruism and solidarity is essentially related to the former, our identification with those who suffer but with whom we have no contact. We feel a desire to help them within the limits of our possibilities, which is sincere in the generous and often hypocritical and false in the selfish.

This selfless help, devoid of power games, which are the topic of this book, shows us how life in society might be if we were more aware of the psychological mechanisms that consume us and make us act like animals. It's not just instinct that stops us from organizing a social order compatible with our intelligence, and certainly in keeping with our interests. We are victims of errors of judgement, age-old errors that are transferred from one generation to the next with little, if any, questioning.

The ability to feel another person's pain, when they are closer to us, is compassion. When it manifests as a selfless will to help (which we usually only see in the event of illness or other tragedies among family or friends), it bears much in common with solidarity. Those who receive help in sincere circumstances like these respond with gratitude, not envy. It is a shame that we see these constructive phenomena so much less than the aggressive and destructive scenario I am describing.

10 Many people think that our genetic affinities with higher mammals — with whom we share something like 98% of our genes — explain some of the attitudes we share with them. Such affinities are supposedly founded precisely on our mammalian peculiarities. Competitiveness, fights over "females", and social inequalities are said to be inevitable characteristics in those who are related to apes, lions, and other animals. While I don't deny that there may be some truth in this, I find myself thinking in the opposite direction: it's incredible how, if only 2% of our genes are different, we are capable of behaving so differently!

We may have instincts similar to those of other mammals. It may be that we are influenced by them and that many of our typical understandings of the structure of our private and social lives are affected — without us being fully aware of it — on such impulses, which arise spontaneously in us. However, what most characterizes us is not this, but our ability to — despite the difficulty — create a language capable of storing and transferring information from one generation to another. With it, we have been able to acquire knowledge and have at our disposal everything our predecessors were able to create, in every sense — artistic, scientific and technological, as well as customs and forms of social organization. We are, therefore, a species with a history. Or, in Ortega y Gasset's somewhat radical statement: "Man has not a nature, but a history" (in his work *History as a System*).

I believe that, thanks to the special development of our brains, we have been able to develop a sophisticated and complex system of reflection and data collection based on memory. We are capable of incredible psychological operations and can make up stories that didn't happen, paint landscapes we haven't seen, and create music that moves us. I find it very hard to see these things — and so many others — as merely part of the chemical activities of our neurons. I have the impression that, at a certain point, human reason (encompassing all of our thought processes and feelings) takes on a life of its own, as if it has become separate from the brain and is even able to influence it — as well as, obviously, continuing to be influenced by it and its conditions of health or illness. Perhaps this explains the body-soul dualism so characteristic of our way of thinking and so hard to abandon. Although I may be criticized for it, because I know this view isn't in vogue, I think it's good to think that we really do have a soul that arises from the autonomy of thought, as opposed to the brain itself. In the computer metaphor I mentioned a few chapters earlier, the brain would be the hardware and the soul, the software. The relationship between them is obvious and, of course, my concern here isn't to discover whether the soul — this immaterial element that characterizes us and enables us to perform all kinds of unique actions — is immortal or not. It is born of the body and we will know in good time if it dies with the body or not.

I have written all this to reaffirm my belief that there is little to be gained in thinking about humankind and its destiny — individual or social — based on what happens with other animals. We are a unique species, indeed. We have a soul and with it we can influence and change our biological predispositions. We are much freer to build an original life than other mammals. We are capable of sophisticated emotions, such as solidarity and compassion. It's a shame we still haven't found a way to make everyone capable of this, an essential condition in order to build a fair social order.

twelve

I think the next step is to try to take these consider-ations — taken essentially from my experience in psy-chotherapy with all kinds of people considered "normal" — into the broader domain of the humanities in gener-al. **The first observation I would like to make based on what I have written can be summed up in the following statement: "evil" comes before "good"; selfishness be-fore generosity. I shall explain: we are born needing to receive everything and without the slightest ability to give back. Unless we are systematically induced and encouraged to change this attitude, we tend to remain in this rather parasitic state of inertia and passivity. Education is thus indispensable to any social group; we are encouraged to learn what is necessary in order to be self-sufficient.** This learning process already im-plies the renouncement of our previously privileged condition — even though this in itself can be considered highly unfavourable when compared to the uterine stage of life! Any learning means, therefore, renounce-ment and requirements that didn't exist before.

Many children are born with lower frustration toler-ance and have a hard time dealing with the education process — which inevitably involves the loss of privileges. They often spend most of their first year of life crying, perhaps disgruntled with the adversities to which they have been exposed since birth. They have great difficulty accepting the norms imposed on them by their social group. They throw tantrums and continue to act impulsively, transforming their intolerance into aggressiveness. If they are unable to overcome this obstacle — the first big one for all of us — their development will stop here.

The interruption of a person's emotional — and moral — development happens when they run into an obstacle they are unable to overcome. As such, children with a lower frustration threshold seize up and stop in the early stages of development. They can't bear the pain inherent to the process of socialization. As the years go by they maintain behaviour typical of 5 or 6-year-old children and persist in their original selfishness — the passivity inherent to their first years of life. They don't control the impulsiveness born of their aggression toward those who impose norms and limitations on them, and they remain incapable of putting themselves in other people's shoes — since this requires that they develop some capacity for suffering, even if only in the realm of the imagination.

I see cruelty as typical of the emotional immaturity caused by the early interruption of the process of socialization. That is, it implies a revolt against social norms — not at all sophisticated and totally inspired by personal limitations derived from low frustration tolerance.

Some twenty years ago I wrote, "Cruelty is born of weakness." The aggressive and impulsive behaviour characteristic of cruel people can give rise to misunderstandings, since it may be treated as the behaviour of someone with a "strong personality". **I have already said that lack of control over one's own feelings is a sign of weakness.** Moreover, people with low pain-thresholds tend to take a cowardly stance in situations of risk, since failure implies great suffering. In practice, these people avoid directly competitive situations, are fast to quit activities when they run into obstacles, and avoid more intense romantic involvement, etc. They may pose as strong and exuberant, but avoiding all situations involving risk is an obvious weakness.

Clearly, this kind of behaviour leads them further away from becoming self-sufficient (here, as always in psychology, there are countless exceptions). Even as adults, they are complacent about their limitations and try to obtain whatever they lack from the generous in a parasitic manner. Again, **I must stress that there are degrees of selfishness, which implies degrees of cruelty. Cruelty in a pure state is rare, fortunately. The fear of reprisal, which is also a kind of psychological pain, makes most of the selfish operate within certain limits, respecting many social norms. It is not uncommon for them to exercise their selfishness more explicitly in their more intimate relationships — with parents, siblings, spouses, business partners, and even children. It is interesting and important to note that cruel behav-**

iour in the domestic sphere often remains invisible to the majority, and is rarely subject to social reprisal, except in the rare cases where physical violence (including rape) is reported, which is uncommon even today.

In short, I believe cruelty is characterized by the lack of an internal braking mechanism that limits human actions. These inner brakes, related to fear and shame, do not limit adequately, because people often act impulsively in ways that disrespect or even harm the rights of others. Their actions, however, can be so subtle that they pass below the radar of social reprisal. The behaviour of people who only respond to external limiting factors depends solely on such boundaries, and we all know that at certain moments in the history of nations there can be a kind of suppression of the norms that limit aggressive behaviour. I am referring, for example, to the condition of a country at war, a situation in which homicidal aggression toward the "enemy" becomes not only acceptable, but virtuous. This was true of Nazism, religious movements such as the Inquisition, and so many other moments in our bloody history in which cruelty has been absolutely banal and epidemic.

13
thirteen

I feel I must, once again, state my perplexity and indignation at psychoanalytical postulates that take for granted the universal existence of a "superego". Is it possible that shrewd, perspicacious observers of the human psyche, especially Freud and his early disciples, were so dramatically mistaken? Even in the face of what many of them saw in Austria and Germany in the years preceding World War II? I believe so. I know well how difficult it is, even today, to go against such a strongly engrained thought system. I have never managed to be a faithful follower of this or any other doctrine, however, and I strongly believe that, in science, all dogmas are there to be surpassed by new observations. It is a dynamic, interminable, fascinating process.

Everything appears to suggest that the ability to step outside of ourselves and into someone else's shoes, without transferring our own characteristics to them, is quite limited. I imagine that it works something like this: a person who has a superego may find it hard to understand someone who doesn't (because they are different). This can be further complicated by the fact that someone who doesn't feel remorse can claim to. One way to solve the problem is to believe that the person acting cruelly isn't fully aware of what they are doing, and that their behaviour is dictated, at least in part, by unconscious emotional imperatives. The interpretations grow in complexity and it may all come down to something very simple: our differences are greater than we are able to comprehend.

Trying to get inside someone else's psyche without bias and free of our own values in order to understand what goes on there is a difficult and risky business. It is similar to what a hacker does when they hack into someone else's computer system to obtain inside information — very different to our usual process of identification, wherein we try to project our own understanding of things onto other people, which leads to all kinds of misunderstandings. It is difficult and the chances of making mistakes are high, although they are smaller than the rather gross error of seeing others in our likeness and image.

This task is absolutely necessary in order to comprehend the true dimension of our differences, even of those who speak the same language, were raised in the same culture and express themselves using the same words. I have said before that terms like "guilt" and "remorse", for example, can be used without the corresponding emotions. "I love you" can be an empty sentence or one of the most intense manifestations of our subjectivity. We are only able to distinguish what is really happening when we pay attention to people's behaviour, coherence and consistency. **In short, people's differences should not be underestimated just because they speak the same words[11].**

One of the "characteristics" of the selfish is their ability to lie with ease. Children learn to lie at around 3 to 4 years of age. It is a dangerous "fruit" of human intelligence, such that it is another element that characterizes us as a species. It is the "discovery" — which must be experienced very vividly — that it is possible to tell a story or describe an action in a different way to what actually happened. Children tend to use this subtle resource, at least in an early phase, to avoid being punished. They may become more "polished" at it and start doing it to obtain undue benefits. In this case, we are clearly within the realm of selfishness. When they start to recognize the rights of others, children tend to stop lying for personal gain, because this would mean someone getting hurt — as happens when someone receives a benefit that wasn't theirs to receive. In the case of those whose concern for others remains underdeveloped, the ability to lie persists and tends to improve. Once again, it is important to remember that many of these supposedly unconscious processes are perfectly conscious, and seem confusing only because people become more honed in their ability to lie.

11 I believe that the constitution of people's psyches — influenced by the characteristics of their brains, the environments in which they grow up, the details of their personal histories, and the different ways in which they register events — can lead us to the conclusion that we are all unique. Studies of the personality traits of identical twins who grew up in the same environment show this. They are similar in many aspects, as is to be expected. But they also have striking differences, which shows that small individual events and the way each one thinks, different from the start, can lead to differences by no means insignificant. There are cases of identical twins in which one is homosexual and the other, heterosexual, as well as cases in which one is selfish and the other, generous.

These data show, once again, that historical and cultural factors take precedence over our genetic makeup. I consider the evidence to be so obvious and unquestionable that I am constantly surprised by the number of colleagues who really believe we are products of our brain chemistry.

I also think it is interesting that people often want to minimize differences. They seem to feel good and safe when they think of other human beings as "brothers", creatures who feel and think in a similar way. Everything suggests that we don't really like to recognize our uniqueness in these essential aspects — though we love to be different in more superficial ones, fuelling our vanity — because it leads us to a painful feeling of loneliness. Similar points of view and behaviour traits make us feel safe, while differences and diverging opinions make us feel alone and unprotected. There's little point fighting the facts. No matter what the pain we must deal with, the truth is that, strictly speaking, we are all condemned to what Ortega y Gasset called "radical solitude" (*Man and People*).

14 fourteen

Children are almost completely dependent when they are born. Since they tend to be complacent about this situation, they have to be encouraged to become independent and self-sufficient. At this stage they are neither "good" nor "bad". They are just beings that are finishing their basic development outside of the womb. Those unable to become independent lag behind and have to use every possible resource to continue to survive by leaning on others: they lie, resort to emotional blackmail, intimidate, and use physical strength. They are always seeking benefits they do not have coming, but which are necessary to their survival. They are mean people (differing from one another in degrees and nuances), whose common ground is selfishness and an absence of internalized norms and values.

Those who manage to overcome these first obstacles develop an inner moral sentiment, mainly by imitating the values of the social environment they are growing up in. They learn to put themselves in other people's shoes, and learn that in dire circumstances it is a good idea to waive one's own rights if it will help someone else who appears to be in need. They learn that those who renounce their rights gain kudos, even if unduly. A child who gives his own toy to a sibling who is crying because he wants something that isn't his does so, at least initially, begrudgingly, for fear of the sibling's violent reaction, and out of pity and guilt for his "suffering". He relinquishes it because he is unable to act in any other way.

So far we have a situation that is adequate and, to a degree, understandable: the owner of the toy is being subjected to extortion, as the other child tries to unduly appropriate his toy. The other child will do anything — anything at all — to get it. If the owner of the desired object is unable to resist, he will be the loser. In our culture, most adults watching a scene like this shower praise on the one who just lost his toy! They say he's a good boy because he "gave up" his toy. As such, the child (who experienced the "surrender" as weakness and lack of competence in self-defence) may now feel stronger, superior. He is different to his sibling, and better. His weakness has just been promoted to strength and virtue![12] This is how generosity and its actions, which have to do with kindness and undue personal sacrifice, are born.

Generosity is thus a weakness that has been promoted to a strength. Bad start! We need to try to better understand how this weakness, which makes a child with inner brakes so susceptible to external pressure, comes about. Since the late 1970's I have been mulling over the importance of dissecting the origins of generosity from a psychological point of view, for reasons which (I hope) are becoming clear, and others which will appear later in this book. Armed with more information, we can now reassert that — at least from a chronological point of view — generosity comes after selfishness ("good" after "evil"). It comes into being as the inability to resist the pressure of selfishness. It is born as a weakness in a social order that makes it a virtue, a strength.

It is possible that, if the social norm were different, many children in the situation described above would be able to resist these pressures. If, instead of being patted on the back for their undue sacrifice and told they are good, they were better informed about what was going on and encouraged to not give in, we would no doubt be looking at a very different individual and social scenario. In order for the social environment as a whole and the members of each family group in particular to act reasonably, they would have to be able to overcome similar processes to which they were subjected during their formative years. There would have to be a dramatic break, since the social world is made up of people whose behaviour embodies a thought system and beliefs developed in previous eras.

---

12 I must register my debt here to Nietzsche, whose *On the Genealogy of Morals* and *Beyond Good and Evil* I read while writing this book. In addition to the extraordinary pleasure of reading such beautiful texts, I confess I have been influenced by this incredible thinker, who was a scathing critic of Christian generosity and rather disapproving of warriors — whom I do not admire either. Nietzsche also talked about the importance of beliefs, which are handed down from previous generations as ready-made norms, crystallized around ideas of God and religion, which impose limits on natural human behaviour. It isn't my intention here to comment on his reflections. I just want to state here that reading his books has influenced me.

15 fifteen

Contemporary psychology has missed a golden opportunity to try to interfere and bring about changes in these beliefs. On the contrary, in some ways it reaffirms and validates the existence of this dual behaviour pattern. It recognizes selfishness as immaturity, but seeks rather superficial explanations for its presence in people's adult lives. Explanations about particularly painful experiences during their formative years are standard — but not always true, since it is not a fact that the selfish have, as a rule, suffered more traumatic experiences. They have induced us to pity and overprotect them forever, to the detriment of everyone. **The generous may really feel superior and privileged, which means they have a greater duty to help the selfish, "poor things", scarred by childhood "traumas". Psychology continues to confirm, with new words, the notion that generosity is a virtue which implies obligations that favour the selfish. Some gain undue benefits, others, undue applause and praise.**

It is important to remember the influence of vanity on our private lives. Its interference in our moral makeup is so dramatic that it is able to make the downtrodden feel privileged. We are so sensitive to praise — and also get addicted to it — that even when we are aware of every facet of a process such as this, we have a hard time acting differently. ("Addiction" means we can't change our behaviour even when we know we must.) When we stand up for our rights, we feel diminished, humiliated, weakened. As time goes by, if we are not careful, we are less and less bothered about having to give up something that is ours, and more and more gratified by the feeling of superiority and power thus obtained. **We feel increasingly strong and superior because we are able to cope with more and more exploitation and abuse without feeling terribly hurt! Not all that different to the deeply pious who used to take joy in self-flagellation.**

The generous start to believe that they will be well liked, even loved, because of this "virtue". They believe that, because of their social acceptance and the envy they inspire in the selfish, they have reached a higher level of evolution. **I am not denying that generosity is emotionally more advanced than selfishness.** However, if we follow this reasoning, it would appear that the more generous a person is, the greater their emotional maturity. This is not just untrue, but it may also be the cause of some of the biggest emotional and interpersonal problems. **If the generous feel loved as a result of their excessive dedication, then, whenever they feel romantically insecure, they will try harder to be even more generous. If the selfish realize that this is how they operate, they will go out of their way to appear increasingly dissatisfied and demanding.** The generous thus live in a constant state of insecurity, because the selfish make it clear that their "love" is conditional to growing dedication and sacrifice, which further heightens their own envy. **We wind up back at the "diabolical story" I mentioned earlier.**

I think it is a big psychological mistake to equate greater generosity with greater emotional maturity, just as I think it is a serious moral error to see supreme generosity as a supreme virtue.

16 sixteen

As I have already written (but do not tire of repeating or trying to imbue with new insights), generosity establishes itself as a result of a new fragility and is reinforced by vanity and the fact that current social beliefs hold it as a virtue. This new fragility arises precisely because the generous are strong and good at putting themselves in other people's shoes. The selfish, incapable of this psychological operation, don't have it. In this new aspect, they are stronger than the generous. But what is this weakness? It is composed of at least two ingredients: the fear of hurting others and the inability to keep feelings of guilt in check.

Fear of hurting others comes from our ability to put ourselves in their shoes. When we hurt them, even when in self-defence or in response to a prior offence, we imagine the pain we cause them. Because we know they have difficulty dealing with suffering, we take pity on them and back down. In this case, the coward is the one who is afraid to lash out because they can't bear feeling they have made someone else suffer, even when they deserve it. We feel pity when we identify with the pain we image the other person is experiencing. And this feeling of pity becomes even more complex — mixed with guilt — if we believe we are the cause of the pain. It is a process which, like everything, involves vanity and a certain feeling of superiority: the other person won't be able to deal with the pain of my response, while I, the stronger one, can handle the suffering and arbitrariness to which they subject me. I take the suffering for myself because I feel superior and better equipped to deal with it; but above all it is because I don't know how to react adequately.

Pity, in its purest and simplest form, is truest when we are in the role of observer. We identify with and are saddened by the suffering of a person whose pain has no direct bearing on us. In processes in which we are personally involved, pity and guilt mix in a way that is difficult to separate. Since we haven't been properly trained to reflect on our emotions and feelings, we often feel pity and guilt when we shouldn't. All it takes is for someone to accuse us of having caused some ill for us to feel bad, even if the person accusing us is a consummate liar. I have already said that the generous feel guilt — or pity — for the simple fact of not having been generous. In other words, if someone makes an absurd request and their answer is no, this is already motive enough for them to recognize traces of selfishness in themselves.

Guilt, a deep, painful sadness, should only be felt in cases in which we really did cause someone else to suffer — intentionally or not. And when we have caused pain unintentionally, we should "forgive ourselves" very quickly, just as, in accordance with the laws that gov-

ern society, unpremeditated crimes are subject to much lighter punishments than premeditated ones. Feeling guilt just because we do isn't right. **We need to reflect deeply on what we are feeling, honestly assessing our responsibility in each circumstance. If we don't, we will make our sophisticated and important inner brakes an enormous source of vulnerability**, making us easy prey for people who have realized that we tend to shoulder the responsibility for crimes we didn't commit. **We make the precious fruit of our evolution (which ensures us, among other things, adequate socialization) into a new weakness.** When this happens, we get stuck, interrupting emotional developments fundamental to our happiness — especially those essential to satisfactory adult romantic relationships.

17

seventeen

Guilt can take on increasingly complex peculiarities and even permeate our entire inner world. One example might be the rather uncommon condition of a girl who has evolved emotionally during her childhood and become generous. When she realizes she is prettier than average, intelligent, and very friendly, she may feel bad for having been favoured by fate in this manner. Her innate characteristics have made her very privileged! She will tend to feel uncomfortable about the envy she inspires in those with fewer natural attributes. She will feel extraordinarily guilty for having innate benefits than can hurt and "offend" others, who are envious of her. Her guilt here is generic and doesn't involve specific faces. It is toward everyone who feels offended, even if unintentionally. We are not talking about deserved or undeserved offences to third parties, but inevitable offences.

What do generous people do in favourable situations like this? They can react in a number of ways, but two are more common. One of these is self-sabotage. They gain weight and use every other possible means to play down their looks, neglecting their hair, skin, clothes, etc. They don't fully develop their intellectual potential, at least in the sense of obtaining success and recognition for their activities. They are just friendly enough to avoid hurting other people's feelings, and avoid any benefit that may come as a result of their qualities. All this to sidestep any discomfort related to envy, which is threatening and uncomfortable. But they also play themselves down so as not to hurt "others", because their envious reaction is preceded by the fact that they feel offended by the presence of something so admirable. Fear and guilt give rise to guarded, discreet behaviour, which yields smaller fruits than the person would otherwise reap — which could also provoke frustration and inner suffering. For far fewer qualities, a selfish person would have embarked on an enormous self-advertising campaign!

Another behaviour, which doesn't exclude the one I have just described, is when generous people become excessively demanding of themselves. **It's as if the fact of having innate privileges implied, above all, greater obligations and duties. Individuals tend to be incredibly devoted to their work and will make great sacrifices for it, as a way of imbuing with "dignity" the privileges they got for free. The pleasure of giving, which characterizes generosity when it is firmly engrained and in tandem with vanity, gains strength and a new ingredient: the pleasant feeling that their achievements are the fruit of great sacrifice and renouncement. The ability to make sacrifices and lead an austere life — even when unnecessary — is perceived as a great moral advance, an undeniable virtue. Sacrifice becomes "vir-**

tue", and enjoying pleasures becomes a "vice". The generous — "virtuous" — feel ashamed when they are living through an extended period in which they don't have to make any kind of special effort. That is, they are unable to enjoy a few days of holidays, even when well deserved, as a reward for enormous prior sacrifices.

The selfish, as is to be expected, do not hesitate to enjoy everything they can reap from innate privileges. If the selfish person is a beautiful girl, she will milk her condition for every possible advantage. She will do the same with her intelligence, friendliness, and social ease. She will use everything she can to make her life as easy and pleasant as possible. The selfish are unfamiliar with the "ethic of sacrifice", so dear to the generous. The selfish are not only unafraid to incite envy in others, but they love to do so. Instead of provoking feelings of guilt, being envied fuels their vanity, since it suggests they are being evaluated positively and seen as superior.

I don't underestimate the envy the selfish may feel at yet another achievement on the part of the generous — being capable of unending sacrifice and effort. But I do think this is another area of confusion, since, in reality, what probably predominates is the envy the generous feel of the selfish. The generous would dearly love to be able to make the most of their privileges: they would love to be free to own the material things that they can afford but which their "moral" modesty rules out; they would love to have the erotic pleasure of showing off physically and awakening the desire of others if it didn't provoke discomfort, a feeling of futility, and the fear of hurting others; they would love to spend days on end doing nothing and not feeling at all guilty about it. What do the generous do when they feel envy? They try to provoke even more envy in the selfish by flaunting their availability, unselfishness, greatness, and superiority. The war between the two types is thus reinforced by one more ingredient; yet another chapter of the "diabolical" story that unites "good" and "evil" is being written.

eighteen

Inciting the envy of someone we envy ourselves is anything but kindness. It is a subtle, discreet, and no less violent form of aggression. We are trying to get our opponent in their weakest spot, their Achilles heel. The selfish, so competent at using and exploiting undue privileges, are perfectly aware that they work like this because they don't have the strength to be self-sufficient. They don't do it because they want to, but because they need to. When the generous supply the selfish with what they need (especially when they do more than is necessary and with great effort and personal sacrifice), they are humiliating the selfish and avenging themselves for the envy they feel, since they don't believe they have the right to enjoy even the things they have generated themselves. **The selfish use what they don't produce and hate it. The generous aren't able to use what they produce and hate it. The selfish hate themselves for it. The generous hate themselves for it. The selfish are deeply envious of the generous. The generous are deeply envious of the selfish.**

The selfish got stuck at life's first obstacle and didn't develop enough frustration tolerance. Their limitations are objective, related to the practicalities of life. The

generous got stuck at the second obstacle and didn't learn to deal adequately with guilt. Their limitations are subjective and have to do with the poor management of feelings generated by their inner moral brakes. The selfish are "bad" because they feel and are weak. The generous are "bad" because they feel and are weak. The generous may not be as weak as the selfish, but they are also weak and lose to the selfish in direct confrontation. **The conclusion is inevitable: generosity is considered "good", and selfishness, "bad" or "evil". However, this assessment is superficial and naïve, because in this case "good" is also "evil". "Good" is a more sophisticated version of "evil".**

Although the conclusion is perplexing, it may explain how this duality, in which one never overpowers or exterminates the other, has managed to survive throughout the millenniums. They are facets of the same process, necessary to one another, constantly reinforcing one another. The vanity of the generous can only be fuelled if the selfish are there to feed off them like parasites. So bring on the selfish, who live off the generous, who, in turn, take pleasure in being needed.

nineteen

The more deeply I reflect on morality, the more shocked and surprised I am at the number of serious mistakes we have made in our evaluation of this issue so fundamental to our private lives and essential relationships. I am also astounded at the serenity with which most thinkers, philosophers, psychologists, and theologists accept the idea that "good" and "evil" are part of an inexorable duality, which they needn't examine any further in order to find a less contradictory solution. If "good" and "evil" are human constructions, shouldn't we consider trying to find a "third way", a single path we can all follow in harmony?

I have devoted myself above all to assessing these issues within family relationships, with a special focus on conjugal relationships. I have described them in several texts and have repeated them here in basic terms. I would now like to look a little beyond individual psychology and venture into the terrain of social relationships. I am all too aware of my limitations, but even so, I am willing to take my chances in a territory in which I am not an expert, but whose difficulties I do not underestimate.

I'm not one hundred percent sure how individual phenomena become standards and norms of life in society, just as I don't know how many of these norms determine individual phenomena. I'm not sure anyone knows exactly how these things work. At any rate, I believe that in smaller human groups, as was the case with city life until not too long ago, it wouldn't be too hard to imagine interaction between individual and social phenomena. I believe that selfishness, that is, the behaviour pattern typical of those who haven't learned to tolerate obstacles, has always existed. I also believe that these people have always tried to obtain what they desired or needed by force — in other words, by physical coercion in the first instance, and then by blackmail and threats of a psychological nature.

The selfish are those who behave in all phases of life — which in the past was much shorter — as children do until a certain age. We are born devoid of values: children, in their games, don't have any reservations about hurting one another, using physical force to resolve their differences, using other children's weaknesses to insult and humiliate them, taking the biggest part of the cake for themselves, lying, etc. Their inner brakes and limits develop as their process of socialization becomes more sophisticated, just as I think that societies, as they become more complex, also began to develop norms to be followed by their members. Childhood punishments, handed out by parents, are substituted in our adult lives by the justice system, which hands out punishments similar to the former in many ways.

Once again I am surprised by the flaws in psychoanalytical thought, which accepts the notion that very young children are capable of feeling guilt. I don't see how guilt can exist in someone who has no internalized moral sentiment, and I don't see any sign of its presence before the age of 5 or 6 in most children. In fact, those who are capable of this internalization become easy prey for those who remain selfish, free of all kinds of restrictions that come to weigh on the generous. The selfish reign in the world of children, and those who are more fearful and delicate from birth don't usually have pleasant memories of this phase, a time when they were deeply humiliated and put down by their peers.

In the same way, it is not unlikely that, in an earlier phase of life in society, the selfish actually felt powerful because they were physically more prepared to fight. Those who managed to become more tolerant were treated as if they were weaker, and were not differentiated from those who acted the same way out of fear — who must have been the overwhelming majority, especially common folk, who, in my mind, don't actively participate in the constitution of the norms and rules of society. The selfish were the masters, and those unable to say "no" to them were the slaves. The slaves, as a group, began to gain some strength as the selfish became increasingly dependent on them, since they generated much of what the masters needed. I think the masters were physically stronger men (who remained selfish), and the oppressed were their women and men who were less aggressive because they were physically less apt, more fearful, or not as good at fending off aggression.

Flávio Gikovate

Intelligence is one of our innate, essential qualities. I imagine there were people of higher intelligence among the selfish as well as the oppressed. It was inevitable that at some stage members of the oppressed would find a solution for their condition, since, I imagine, they were constantly trying to change it. (I shall not attempt, for total lack of qualification, any historical or chronological reconstruction of this society.) It's no surprise, for example, that the slaves developed religious rites in which they felt they could avenge their humiliation. Voodoo rituals against their oppressors were the only possible form of revenge. It also doesn't surprise me that over the centuries women oppressed by their husbands — masters — developed all manner of strategies and ruses to improve their position in unequal relationships, in which physical strength was predominant and used against them.

I don't think it is absurd to suppose that generosity arose among the oppressed, given that self-sacrifice was compulsory — much like what happens with more frail children who find themselves obliged to give away or lend their toys against their will. The oppressed used their intelligence to turn this weakness into a strength, both by associating vanity with the tendency to give and through the growing perception that their oppressors were highly dependent on them, which was their weakness. This gained social acceptance by several means, including reflections of a religious nature, whereby generosity was promoted to strength and virtue — as happened explicitly in Christianity, which promoted this new way of seeing people, in which losers in the game of life became the winners, those who would have access to the kingdom of heaven (Nietzsche). I don't believe religious thought generated this kind of attitude in the oppressed. I believe exactly the opposite: that this idea was born of the intelligence of members of the oppressed and spread because it gained acceptance among them, being a big improvement on their condition. We shouldn't forget that their condition must have been dreadful, such that anything that diminished it or provided relief was very welcome.

From the moment this duality was established between the selfish and the generous (who learned to feel superior through self-sacrifice and their relative power derived from the dependence of the selfish on them) it seems no definitive solution has ever been found for the problem of the strength and weakness of each type. At the end of the day, who is most powerful? Our beliefs — the points of view we internalize without consistent reflection[13] and which are the ready-made legacy of what our ancestors used to think — are jumbled and contradictory. Generosity is supposedly behaviour that is pleasing to God and opens the doors to eternal paradise. However, the best way to enjoy this life is to look out for ourselves and take everything we can for ourselves. Our beliefs praise generosity at the same time as they suggest that it might actually be more convenient to be selfish. The generous practice self-sacrifice here and now and have the advantage in a supposed future life. The selfish do better here and may run into problems in the "next life".

It is important to bear in mind that this is not confusion about any old subject of secondary importance. This is about the forming of a value system, a code that guides individuals in their intimate relationships, as well as in every sphere of social activity. Work-related issues, especially those concerning the division of its fruits, have to be decided according to a set of norms that should determine the conduct of all members of a society. But how do we distinguish between right and wrong if we are unable to reach a consensus about "good" and "evil", generosity and selfishness?

It doesn't surprise me that, in practice, selfishness is predominant among individuals who assume the roles of leaders in social organizations, including today's complex societies, in which the play of economic forces can barely be understood even by the well-informed. This is what ends up happening regardless of the discourse used and the ideas that supposedly define the conduct of a particular group striving to attain power and control the destiny of the people. The selfish always come up trumps when it comes to power since they have no qualms about taking the biggest slice of the cake for themselves. With the selfish, individual interests will always prevail over collective wellbeing.

Are, then, the generous the weaker ones? I don't believe so. The generous are weak in more aggressive disputes. But they are strong, for example, in the gener-

Flávio Gikovate

ation of new ideas. The ability to put oneself in someone else's shoes and deal with abstraction in general is more productive in terms of intellectual creation — which doesn't mean a difference in ability, since intelligence is not exclusive to either the selfish or the generous. I think the generous tend to build a kind of power on the margins of political power that is somehow intertwined with it. In an extreme example, it's as if we had warriors on one side, and priests on the other; political and material power on the one hand, and the power of discourse and ideas on the other. Those who hold the intellectual power furnish those who hold the political power with ideas, such that the latter come to depend on the former. The powerful need to surround themselves with the creative, just as kings and noblemen of the past received philosophers and artists in their courts. Talented, generous people are, in a way, part of the dominant class: they supply the selfish with ideas and receive in return a small portion of the material benefits that they control.

The generous produce new ideas that, as a rule, aim to improve the conditions of the entire community — they also consider the large majority that is excluded from these reflections because their participation in decision-making is limited; even today, in our so-called democratic societies, their participation tends to be manipulated by electoral strategies produced by the elites. Such ideas are twisted and transformed by the selfish elite — who take advantage of the naivety of the people — into instruments of mass oppression. Thus, the beautiful ideas produced by the generous are used to influence the behaviour of the people (the masses), who try to follow them. These beautiful ideas are usually of an ideological or religious nature. The fact is that the elites, made up of powerful selfish people and the generous individuals who keep them in ideas, do not practice what they preach to the people.

The complicity between the generous and the selfish at the top of the social pyramid — probably, as a rule, the most intelligent and clever — strikes me as obvious. They are actually two different kinds of power and vanity, between which an eternal war is waged, precisely as happens between couples in which one is generous and the other, selfish. It is an alliance between two modes of behaviour, both unfair, in which reciprocal favouritism and envy rein absolute. The generous truly believe they have the moral high ground and are representatives of "good", and won't hear of the idea that they practice another form of "evil". The selfish are, in this sense, less dubious; they know they are in possession of the biggest slice of cake and are hungry for more. They see this as legitimate and, as we know, don't feel guilt. At times they may even consider themselves generous, since they occasionally cast crumbs to the less privileged. The generous, because of their guilt, try to resolve their privileges in the ways I have described in other chapters: either by not allowing themselves to enjoy what they have (but which they won't give up for the world!), or by taking on an overload of work — which sometimes affords them even greater rewards, which they do not allow themselves to enjoy.

The result of the reciprocal admiration that unites the generous and the selfish, and the struggle that establishes itself between them through mutual envy, is that they are almost irremediably bound to one another and cannot find a way out of their dilemma. Regardless of the ideas they preach and the discourse they adopt, they generate and always will generate tense and unfair social orders. This is inevitable, because selfishness and generosity are two different kinds of unfairness. Unfair people are not capable of building a fair social order!

13 I would like to state how much I owe to my greatest intellectual influence in more recent years. I am not in the habit of quoting other authors, mostly because my ideas have always been influenced, above all, by my professional work. If I were to register unpayable debts, I would have to pay credit to the almost eight thousand patients I have treated. I cannot, however, neglect to mention the impact of Ortega y Gasset's books on me. One in particular, which is not one of his better-known works, fascinates me tremendously. It is his series of lectures "Ideas y creencias"[2], in which he masterfully demonstrates how we so often think simplistically, merely repeating formulas we have learned and adopted as ours without due critical assessment. Beliefs are many, but ideas are few and far between.

For any attempt at change we need to succeed in freeing ourselves of our beliefs. This isn't easy, because they function as our intellectual foundation, the basis of a psychological structure that sustains us at the same time that it impoverishes us. Our beliefs reassure us, prevent us from having to live with doubt. As Ortega y Gasset said, our intellectual vigour is directly related to our ability to cope with doubt. We tend to prefer quick, simple explanations to the pain of living with doubt. However, human creativity depends on our willingness to experience the state of discomfort of not having all the answers, and managing, at some stage, to have new ideas — rather than just trotting out old beliefs with pomp and ceremony.

---

2 "Ideas and Beliefs" in *What is Knowledge,* trans. Jorge Garcia-Gomez, State University of New York Press, 2002.

twenty

The complexity of the social world both surprises me and becomes more and more palpable as I write these lines. I don't think it is possible to take what can be learned from analyzing more intimate interpersonal relationships (my area of specialty) and transfer it to our social interactions. The social dimension implies new variables that I can only guess at, since I am not an expert on the subject. I don't know how to clearly assess, for example, the forming of the elites, the minority who prevail over the masses, the "silent majority" who accept their condition perhaps because they have had less formal education; perhaps due to a docility handed down through generations of oppressed ancestors; perhaps even because many have no intention of being part of any elite — since less vain people may also be less ambitious and think so differently that we sometimes have a hard time understanding them.

I believe that the big difference in behaviour between the general population and the elites is related to vanity — the desire to stand out from the crowd that is common to all, but much more intense in some. There is likely a relationship between the intensity of a person's vanity, the way it manifests, and their intelligence[14].

The vanity of the intellectually less sophisticated manifests in a simpler way and requires less to be satisfied, while the vanity of the more intellectually sophisticated requires more complex reinforcement that is harder to attain. **The elites love to call attention to themselves for rare properties (intellectual, aesthetic, or material), while the general population is content receiving attention for much less. The elites demand of themselves ways of being, thinking, and living that are off limits for most of the population — what i refer to as "aristocratic pleasures".** The general population is content with a lifestyle that is no different to that of their neighbours — they seek "democratic pleasures". In my professional experience, essentially focused on analyzing the subjectivity of the elites, I haven't seen evidence that those at the top of the social pyramid are any happier or more serene, or enjoy greater wellbeing. On the contrary, they are always competing, overly concerned with keeping up with the Joneses.

The generous who are part of a social elite are so because of their ability to stand out for intellectual aptitudes, whether suited to corporate employment or not. They are often teachers, independent professionals, small or medium-sized business owners, "good" folks who have pursued social success driven by vanity and personal ambition. They often have to conceal such ambitions from themselves, camouflaging them in collective ideals of a political, religious, or even scientific or artistic nature. I am saying that most successful generous people are drawn to these fields — not that most of those who work in these professional areas are generous. I know all too well that many of those who work in these areas are very selfish — although there is no way of knowing what percentage. For them, personal ambitions are explicit and needn't be disguised. Disguises are only necessary to dodge the rigid, internalized moral sentiments of the generous.

I have used the word "elites" in the plural to refer to those at the top of the social pyramid because I believe it is always important to separate the generous from the selfish, who make up independent "elites". The members of the generous elite live side by side with those who directly seek material success, eminence, and social distinction, as well — of course — as political power. The selfish are more objective and seek to achieve their goals without self-deception. They work in professions that offer quick rewards, and don't feel compelled to act in accordance with the moral values taught by the official discourse of their field. This group of people, those who work in areas more focused on practical results of a material nature, also includes some generous individuals who, early on, acquire a slightly more realistic vision of life in society. They are substantially fewer in number to the selfish "infiltrated" in professions of an intellectual nature.

The selfish are freer to use trickery and take advantage of the positions they occupy without reservation. They can be found in the world of big business, politics, and

highly profitable illegal activities (gambling, drug traf-
ficking), etc. Those who are successful seek results with
determination and effort (uncommon qualities among
the selfish, and almost entirely exclusive to the successful
ones), and usually get better results than the generous,
since they can exercise their ambition more directly.

I think, socially speaking, the selfish tend to do better
than the generous: they appropriate their ideas and use
them for their own benefit. They are capable of "steal-
ing" ideas, "cheating" while vying for positions at work,
"pocketing" money by exploiting the benefits of a particular professional position. They are capable of this and
much more, precisely because they don't feel guilt. They
are winners in any kind of face-to-face dispute — and the
same thing happens in their family lives. Generous people with the same dose of ambition will lose the dispute
because of self-imposed limitations arising from their inability to harm others even when they are disloyal. They
are unable to meet disloyalty with disloyalty, and so lose
even when they are more capable. They lose and allow
hurt and anger to build up inside them, which will eventually generate some kind of retaliation.

The generous use their weapons — creativity and a
subtler, more sophisticated intellect — to show off and
stand out in the eyes of the selfish. They provoke their
envy, even though they don't know that this is what
they are doing. They feel intellectually superior! The
selfish, incited by this envy, go about flaunting their
glories and material conquests, which are treated with

disdain and superiority by the generous, as if they didn't care for expensive adornments and objects. The selfish are materialists, while the generous are more drawn to the intellectual world. Obviously, I am simplifying things here for the purpose of illustration; many people, in fact, like to seek distinction through both means and provoke universal envy[15].

---

14 Everything I manage to write and think about human vanity will pale in comparison with the importance of this sentiment that accompanies us for most of our lives and which inebriates and addicts us. Those who grow accustomed to some kind of fame usually can't let go of it without great suffering. This happens even when the fame brings hostilities born of envy or the invasion of privacy. The most interesting thing is that vanity seems to lay siege especially to more intelligent individuals. This isn't because they have a stronger sexual impulse, which I believe to be the source of the original sentiment — which makes a child of 8 or 9 years of age feel eroticized when they use a new physical adornment such as a watch or necklace.

I think that vanity — the vague erotic pleasure derived from attracting the attention of others — permeates our intellectual processes to produce a final emotion connected to practically all aspects of our subjectivity — which would explain the line in Ecclesiastes, "Vanity of vanities; all is vanity." This yearning for distinction seems to contaminate above all the most intelligent minds in a way that is not even clear to them, an indication that intelligence isn't always accompanied by adequate self-assessment. People with strong feelings of guilt and humanitarian ideas tend to exercise their vanity through simplicity, which can create the impression that they have managed to tame this peculiar aspect of their sexuality. In reality, they seek attention in this manner just like those who flaunt wealth, power and luxury. Once again, there are two kinds of elite: those who seek to stand out for their wealth and things they consider more attractive, and those who appear to look down upon the former — in itself a different kind of distinction, which makes them feel superior and less futile.

The forms of expression of vanity are diverse, including those characterized by intellectual exhibitionism. Many materially frugal individuals love to display their knowledge and uncommon aptitudes. They seek distinction in other areas, but according to the same criteria, seeking to be better, superior, or more capable than their peers. I believe, and have for over twenty years, that vanity is unquestionably the emotion

Flávio Gikovate

that most stimulates competition among us, since it is at the root of that which we call ambition. Ambition is a way of thinking and feeling that validates the desire to be better than most, to top oneself and one's competitors. Our society clearly defends ambition and competitiveness. The saddest part is that those who criticize the competitive nature of our kind of social organization are also ambitious and fight for distinction in their areas in exactly the same way. In other words, those who would like to change the rules of the game of life in society feel and act in exactly the same way as those they criticize. It is to be expected that the outcome is eternal repetition and that the alternance of power in societies with very similar elites ends up in much of a muchness.

I dream — and know very well I won't live to see it — of the day in which more intelligent people decide to enjoy life in a different manner, serenely seeking activities compatible with their interests, acting cooperatively rather than competitively. I dream of the arrival of this day at least in places that should be a true haven of knowledge, such as universities. I dream, although I know perfectly well that it means human vanity will have to have been tamed and domesticated, and that these future individuals won't even have been touched by it, much less felt the magnitude of its influence on their thoughts and behaviour.

15

I have said before that I have always found it hard to understand how the essential processes of life in society take place. I think the last 150 years have been marked by important discoveries in the sciences, and that they have led to technological advances that have dramatically interfered with our habitat. We know that most of our private life is governed by beliefs that are, in general, conservative, creating a tendency to repeat the patterns we have been taught. Artists and scientists are usually better able to deal with doubt, such that from their minds "spring" new ideas that can become concepts and doctrines capable of generating technological innovations. Thus, the steam engine was invented, giving rise to ships and trains able to travel faster than horses (horsepower being a standard measure of engine power still in use).

This change in the speed of locomotion facilitated communication between societies that had previously been more isolated. Along came electricity and nights took on a new meaning. Then someone invented photography, cinema, and television, just to cite a few things that have had a great influence on our day-to-day lives. Not to

▶

mention computers and so many other inventions that have quickly multiplied by the million (and billion) thanks to the economic interest these innovations spark in entrepreneuring spirits, completely different to those who generated the original ideas — the eternal alternance between the two elites.

Advances have been made in biology, which have had repercussions in medicine, life expectancies, and new issues related to activities for the elderly, who used to be an exception but are now becoming the rule. The contraceptive pill was invented, bowling down age-old beliefs about the importance of a girl's virginity before marriage. Even the walls of the traditional family structure have crumbled, family being less and less necessary, since the pill has freed women to go to the workplace, along with machines that have taken over most activities requiring strength. In other words, it is impossible to sustain beliefs about anything at all. The period we have been living through, which we all know and of which the facts I have cited are just more vivid examples, has brought the inevitable ruin of beliefs, accompanied by strong feelings of destitution, insecurity, and depression — for which science has hurried to find new remedies, which, evidently, figure among the top selling products of our time.

In other words, certain restless spirits have invented new things and others have transformed them into consumer goods with which they make fortunes and accrue power. These new goods interfere with the behaviour and lifestyles of people in general, obliging them to break with their beliefs. This all takes place as if by chance, without control. I don't believe there are influential people who could have foreseen the consequences of more recent discoveries. Everyone complains of growing individualism in the social world. But how could things be different if we now have TVs, computers, and MP3 players, to name just some of the devices capable of entertaining us individually? Families complain that their children are starting their sex lives earlier and earlier, but how could this be different if there is contraception — and if TV programs and films are always advertising the pleasures of sex?

I feel that all control has been lost over human life processes in society, if indeed we ever were in control of them. I don't know if we have always been adrift and doctrines and explanations have always come *a posteriori* (as I believe happens today), or if this is a more recent phenomenon. Is it possible that when change came more slowly and gradually there was more time to anticipate the consequences of each new acquisition? Is it possible advent of printed books and newspapers caused a similar impact to the invention of television? I am unqualified to even try to answer such questions. It strikes me as obvious, however, that what most interferes in our beliefs and obliges us to change even when our tendency is to be

▸

complacent is the emergence of new ideas in the sciences and their transformation into new devices capable of substantially changing our habitat, to which we are forced to adapt.

This inexorable adaptation to our new physical environment probably sets off a series of internal changes that are processed imperceptibly. The growing individualism about which so many of us complain is being processed inside each and every one of us. Nowadays people speak of choosing romantic partners based on affinities and it appears everyone has already forgotten the time — not so long ago — when people thought exactly the opposite. These are just examples of inner changes brought about by changes in the outside world as a result of human scientific progress. It is possible that, even by chance, interesting and important advances arise from these processes, which are beyond all control.

21
twenty one

The lower classes have little to do with this whole story. The selfish and the generous can also be found here. I believe the differences in their personality types are more apparent in their private lives, in which the selfish (sadists), are cruel to the generous (masochists), who take pleasure in suffering, which makes them feel stronger and more tolerant. In the social arena, the generous may be more fervently religious, faithfully living according to their creeds. The selfish are always more hypocritical, such that disloyalty and misdemeanours are run-of-the-mill to them. When caught, they are punished according to the justice system of the elites — to whom it is rarely applied.

It is never easy to show the generous that their attitudes are underpinned by weaknesses, however, it is easier to convince them that this is true in their private lives than in their public activities. The generous can see that, in their private lives, they tend to give in when in a tight spot. But they are very resistant to the idea that there is an important element of self-interest in their public activities, whether in direct political action or any other social activity to which they devote themselves with dedication and self-sacrifice. The generous believe themselves to be propelled and motivated by their convictions and ideals and can't — or don't want to — see anything beyond this.

They consider themselves decent folk, different in every way to the selfish — the "bad guys". People whose political ideals are centred on attempts to build an egalitarian world are often blind to the fact that they live in complete disharmony with their convictions. Oddly enough, when the evidence of such a radical contradiction is so great that they can no longer deny it, they become evasive, as if their discourse were more important than the house they live in. They say that individual sacrifice would be in vain and wouldn't bring about any relevant social change, political practice supposedly being the way to do so. No one is obliged to live in a palace, and those who argue for a simpler lifestyle — accessible to most of the population — could live as they preach. Examples are worth more than words.

The truth is that differences between the lifestyles of the generous and selfish elites are much smaller than one would expect judging from what they say. Rhetorical differences tend to define the two large political blocks: one explicitly defends social inequality, which they attribute to differences in individual potential defined according to the laws of nature that govern all animal life on the planet; while the other group believes we have logic and discernment, and that these ingredients, the fruit of our unique, sophisticated minds, can be used to build a better human society,

built in accordance with values that we can create for ourselves — such that we do not need to copy the original laws of the jungle.

I have no qualms about positioning myself with those who believe that our species — though it has much in common with certain other mammals — has a privileged brain, capable of completely changing our biological destiny. However, I cannot ignore the facts, especially events I have witnessed in my lifetime, about the arrival in public power of those who defend beautiful ideas. These people undergo rapid metamorphoses and the result is almost always disappointing. It seems that power completely changes people's conduct. Given that, in practice, the elites have always lived in a similar manner to one another, everything seems to suggest that these similarities grow deeper the closer they are to power. This alone should be enough to prompt the generous to put their convictions and ideals in check; they should question more rigorously the consistency of their behaviour and the extent to which it actually differs from that of those they criticize so scathingly.

I am not trivializing the concrete facts and the objective conditions of large-scale social processes, nor do I underestimate the pressure on well-intentioned politicians to sell out on their convictions. I won't go into this now. I would merely like to stress, once again, what I have noted in my psychological observations: in practice, the actions of the generous in the public sphere are much more similar to those of the selfish than they care to think. In power, the similarities are even greater. Everything leads me to believe that, in both the private and public spheres, there is something very wrong in this polarization of "good" and "evil". We cannot expect much in the way of concrete change in these essential areas of life as long as we are unable to unravel this knot and find more consistent solutions to moral dilemmas.

twenty two

So, what can we expect of the near future? Can we hold out any hope that the "alliance" between "good" and "evil" will be broken? How might this take place? Sadly, I have to say that my observations don't allow me to nurture even the slightest amount of optimism (even though optimism is much more comfortable for me, in keeping with my intrinsic approach to life). But in almost forty years of intensive, systematic work as a psychotherapist, I have rarely witnessed significant changes in the moral conduct of patients. The few who changed were those who managed to leave behind their original selfishness and evolve toward generosity. That is, they changed sides. They were not able to go beyond this and complete the cycle of emotional development that had been interrupted. They ended up with the behaviour pattern — also not fully mature — of those who had developed inner moral brakes. They admired the generous and went to great lengths to become one.

From an educational point of view, I haven't seen any kind of change either: children and teenagers continue to be exposed to this dual morality, both at home and at school, such that, when they grow up, they become one type or the other. The models with which they identify have not changed, which leads to the perpetuation of the existing pattern. Patterns change with great difficulty, as much in biology (where some kind of genetic interference through mutation is necessary) as in culture (where beliefs tend to remain the same unless something very extraordinary happens). In all of the environments they inhabit, children come across people who are selfish and generous, good and bad. It is thus inevitable that they also come to be part of one of the two "groups".

If it is so difficult for adults to change — in all aspects, but especially with regards to their moral conduct — and children rarely create new behaviours, since they generally imitate what they observe, it is hard to be terribly optimistic. The only consistent solution, from the point of view of a social group as a whole, not just on an individual level, resides in a change of attitude on the part of the generous, which may now be somewhat easier as a result of the technological advances that have stimulated individualism — which, in this aspect, is welcome. As I wrote earlier, when the selfish evolve, they evolve toward generosity, an attitude they lacked during their formative years. Those who are capable of this metamorphosis become easy prey for the selfish who have not changed (the majority), since both guilt and the recently acquired taste for self-sacrifice make them act like the generous; they can sometimes even be quite "radical". Which really isn't necessary, because, after all, having once been selfish, they are more than familiar with the ruses of those pressuring them.

The "traditionally" generous and the radical "recent-converts" cannot resist the pressure of the selfish and are uncomfortable with this fact. It appears, however, that the feeling of superiority derived from the capacity for self-sacrifice has become an even greater pleasure[16]. They know they are being exploited and feel stronger in spite of it, with a surplus of energy and earnestness. They may, at times, feel silly, but most of the time they feel rich, strong, and powerful. It is a position that brings with it a certain amount of humiliation, but it is fuel for vanity; humiliation appears to be necessary and desirable in order to refuel the entire process.

We need to keep a closer eye on these processes, in which the same action can give rise to antagonistic feelings, such as humiliation and a heightened sense of vanity at the same time. This puts us in a rather complex dilemma, because we are acting in accordance with the values held as superior by our culture, which make us feel proud, virtuous and strong. But our inner voice tells us we are being unfairly exploited, wasting our money, time or energy on someone who doesn't deserve it. If we think more carefully about it, we may be able to find a solution for this process, which, all else aside, is self-perpetuating, since each insult to one's vanity requires new praise.

What might be the solution for this dilemma? It would be for people to try to be less generous. Let's see what happens when they are able to carry through with it and tolerate the guilt associated with the fact that they are not making all of the concessions asked of them (although they are still making some): their vanity is somewhat wounded, because they are often accused of being "selfish" by those who are frustrated by this withdrawal of generosity. The generous are deeply offended when they are accused of being selfish — despite the fact that they sometimes envy the selfish. Their vanity is wounded because the amount of self-sacrifice has been reduced and they have grown accustomed to being one of the "good guys" and being seen as such. Their relative frustration at being exploited remains, because they haven't managed to say a definitive, radical "no". The result isn't positive; the generous end up with their vanity wounded, doubting their right to be so unwavering with others, and somewhat uncomfortable about the concessions they are still making. They end up with the negative aspect of their condition and lose the positive aspect. They convince themselves that the partial withdrawal of generosity is not the solution.

---

16 The pleasure of self-sacrifice is similar to, in the sphere of erotic intimacy, the pleasure of submission and subservience in masochism. It is no accident that Erich Fromm (*The Art of Loving*) said relationships between opposites were sadomasochistic, in which the sadist was the selfish one, and the masochist, the generous one. Some find a curious erotic pleasure in serving and subjugating themselves, as if this position implied a subtle form of domination and power. I believe that once again we are looking at the direct interference of vanity; in other words, the position of inferiority is experienced as power and, therefore, superiority. In my mind, the fact

▸

that pleasure is derived from self-sacrifice doesn't imply moral virtue, but shows that vanity has attached itself here, giving rise to a positive feeling in a process that perhaps, more than anything, should be characterized by humiliation, that is, an insult to one's vanity.

The psychological processes of these people are curious and subtle. It doesn't mean — at least in my opinion — that such complexity gives rise to mechanisms that elude the conscious mind. I don't think of them as something that we receive ready-made, imposed on us through the subconscious. One of my greatest objectives with this book is precisely to try to trace the routes we have forged, deliberately or not, in order to find ways to better position ourselves in relation to other people. The routes we have are the best we have been able to build; they constitute what we have been able to do given the subjective and objective information we have and the magnitude of our emotional competence. It may be that in many cases we would like to act differently. This doesn't mean we are subject to unconscious pressures, but to the limits that preside over us and stop us from overcoming certain obstacles.

23 twenty three

If the solution isn't less, maybe it's more. In this case the generous may become even more generous. The humiliation of feeling abused grows, as does the erotic pleasure of vanity and the feeling of superiority because they believe themselves to be stronger and richer. These movements renew the interest of the selfish, whose envy, fuelled by these new benefits, grows and becomes more explicit. This change doesn't bring wonderful results, but perhaps the overall result is favourable for the generous, because the envy they provoke is a kind of revenge, and their newly-fuelled vanity outweighs their constant feeling of humiliation. Provoking envy, as we know, is a subtle and somewhat cowardly way of settling scores, popular among those who are unable to act in a direct manner because of their guilt.

This radicalization of generous behaviour leads to the radicalization of selfishness, which only increases the feeling of being at a dead end and justifies a less-than-optimistic outlook on the future. The generous — the only ones capable of initiating the process of breaking this duality and the endless duel our existence has become — find themselves increasingly stuck in their behaviour patterns and slaves to vanity,

but feeling powerful and virtuous because their actions are consistent with social and religious beliefs.
Feelings of humiliation are often rewarded by religious
faith, which promises the kingdom of heaven.

Even when we are fully aware of the dimension and
complexity of a human problem, I don't think it is productive or appropriate to consider it unsolvable. I have
sometimes felt this way when dealing with issues related to sexuality: the sexual differences between men and
women appeared to instate a game of power that irremediably condemned us to a permanent war of the sexes.
Recent research, however, has shown that patterns are
beginning to change — even those with a biological basis.
Therefore, not even the limits of our biology should be
treated as something set in stone. In morality, we are dealing with human beliefs, perhaps as hard to change as our
instincts. Nevertheless, it is incumbent on us not to give up
and to look for possible solutions, even if they require a lot
of hard work and take a long time to come to fruition.

I think the solving of our dilemma will have to centre
on changes in the private lives of those aware of the
need for change. I also think that when enough individuals have acquired the competence to embrace a
new way of life (as long as it is better, more consistent,
and gratifying), it will start to affect society, generating
a wave of change. I don't believe the opposite is possible: social changes, ushered in by rational changes
in minority discourse, will never be able to solidify and
interfere in individual behaviour.

The process will have to be initiated by the generous: they are the ones who will have to radically renounce their condition — there is no room, as we have seen, for half-measures. The generous will have to do this even if it brings, at least in the first instance, a sense of loss, reduced value, seriously wounded vanity — and perhaps even wounded self-esteem.

It is important to remember that vanity and self-esteem are completely different psychological processes[17]. Vanity requires observers, or "others", who look at us with admiration or contempt. Self-esteem depends on one's self-assessment. It is an intrapsychological process and, in essence, doesn't depend on others. If a person believes it is good to be generous and dedicated (even when not in the company of others who share these traits), they feel diminished when they fail to act as such and develop a negative self-image — even when others seem to approve of their behaviour.

Self-esteem depends on things that people determine for themselves (different to obeying externally-imposed rules, typical, for example, of military discipline); when not upheld their own self-assessment is what suffers. It thus depends on their ideas and convictions. At times it may go hand in hand with vanity, when one's ideas are in tune with one's goals to inspire the admiration of others. For example, if I truly believe that my value as a human being depends on my physical appearance and the extent to which I can attract the interest of others, especially in romantic issues, my self-esteem will depend on the same results that feed my vanity.

Although their objectives may coincide, it is important that we see self-esteem and vanity as distinct. **Self-esteem depends on the way a person thinks and vanity really depends on what others think. Unfortunately, most of us are not all that creative in our thinking and are dependent on the behaviour and thought patterns of those around us, even though many of the convictions held by other people — not to mention our own — have been received without reflection from previous generations. For most people, self-esteem and vanity have become so confused that they think by undergoing plastic surgery they will be improving their self-esteem.**

---

17 When the generous make an effort not to be so generous, expressions of displeasure from those who have always taken advantage of their generosity can be a blow to their vanity. They are treated as if they were changing for the worse and becoming selfish. They are treated like this by the selfish themselves, who, out of sheer opportunism, try to reinforce their old, convenient behaviour pattern (after all, they have something to lose). If the generous are not deeply convinced that this is exactly what they should be doing, if they waver in their convictions, their self-esteem is also wounded. This is because a person's self-esteem requires that they act in accordance with their convictions, which shouldn't be affected by outside repercussions.

However, if the generous are able to overcome this initial obstacle and continue to face their big internal obstacles (such as undue guilt, fear of abandonment and fear of other reprisals), they will be rewarded with a great feeling of wellbeing, even joy. This feeling of victory is accompanied by what we can call inner pride, for having managed to triumph over a dramatic inner obstacle, for having been able to move toward their ideals as human beings. In this case, their self-image improves — and this is what we should truly call self-esteem. They can enjoy a great sense of wellbeing and intimate satisfaction, even when subject to the criticism and disapproval of those around them. It is an important moment, which may help them see more categorically how little self-esteem has to do with vanity, and how, in many situations, it is even in complete opposition to it.

I don't think letting go of our convictions to please our partners is worth it, under any circumstance. This doesn't mean we can't compromise. We can, and should, in many situations; we can either make concessions in keeping with our convictions or because we don't know how to say no. They are two different things: the former doesn't harm our self-esteem, because we are acting in accordance with it; in the latter situation we are being coerced, unable to resist an external pressure, which is a weakness and, for this very reason, harmful to our self-esteem. We must take great care, because our self-esteem is our greatest asset. It should not be given up even for the most beautiful and significant feelings and emotions. Not even for love, or rather, not even for fear of losing the love of someone important to us; in fact, how can we allow someone who asks us to do something in any way demeaning to be important to us?

twenty four

In our society, to be generous is to have a virtue, even if it is not cultivated by most of our leaders. Generosity is held as a value as much by the dominant religions of the West as by official pedagogical discourse. Most of the children and teenagers who follow this model for the psychological reasons I have already described are convinced of it, and it is also reinforced by an increase in self-esteem because they belong to the "stronger" group. **They are deeply convinced that generosity really is a virtue, such that any transgression has an immediate negative repercussion on their self-esteem — a feeling of debasement, even when there are no observers. Since generosity wins the admiration of many, their vanity is also reinforced. This alliance between self-esteem and vanity is a decisive factor in the perpetuation of this behaviour pattern.**

For vanity to make a significant contribution to the change I am proposing, that is, the radical renouncement of generosity and the end of our age-old duality, social values would need to change before individual ones, and we would need external influence and encouragement to revisit our points of view. We would begin to change in order to acquire new values so we could continue to be admired by our peers. Changes that affect us from the outside in are always, inexorably, related to the impact they will have on our vanity. In this scenario, we would change the way we think as we might change the way we dress, all because of a new "trend" that seduces us and makes us want to keep pace with the group to which we belong.

Because I have never put much faith in this possibility, I doubt that social — and socioeconomic — changes will (or should) precede individual ones. I don't underestimate the power and autonomy of social norms within the laws of psychology. Social change, however, would depend on the coming to power of a sophisticated, subtle elite (that remained so), and that is something I have never believed in! I have always thought that if people had to choose between a belligerent, insensitive general and a gentle, respectful commander, when push came to shove the general would get the power. I think it is easier for the selfish to hold political power. And even when the opposite happens, experience has shown me that power is a rare condition in which generous individuals are capable of undergoing drastic changes and becoming selfish.

25

twenty five

We are left with the opposite alternative, which I find more attractive because it can be put in practice immediately by those who want to: we should strive to change from the inside out, taking advantage of the curious age we are living through, in which our beliefs are being deeply shaken as a result of so many dramatic changes to our social and physical environment. The first step would be to convince ourselves intellectually that the selfish–generous duality is a destructive pact that gets us nowhere. We have to be truly convinced that it is a huge mistake, thousands of years old, transferred to us by social beliefs, and that it is now time to leave it behind and move forward, without sadness or nostalgia. Perhaps my endless repetition throughout this book will help convince people, approaching the topic from many different angles in order to dispel any doubts they may have while reading. We need to be able to disqualify the beliefs that have guided our moral reflection, which is always complicated, because it seems pretentious to want to tamper with such deeply entrenched norms. We must understand the ominous consequences in essential aspects of everyday life: our intimate and professional relationships.

Flávio Gikovate

The second step would be to envisage a new way of thinking and acting, a new vision of moral life to take the place of the old one. This search will have to be more serious and consistent than, say, looking for a new intellectual discourse. We must find norms to inform a new way of behaving and relating to one another. We need to imagine ourselves living differently and like what we imagine in order to find the strength and determination to persist with it. I say this for two reasons. Firstly, because I don't put much faith in beautiful ideas that take a long time to come to fruition — like fruit that rots before it can be eaten. And, secondly, because we have to be determined and steadfast to be able to survive the difficulties that will present themselves along the way. **Although, intellectually, the solution seems simple (elementary even), it is much harder in practice, because it implies a radical break with our individual and social history.**

If taking a new, more appropriate direction were easy, many of us would already have done so. The simplest path isn't always the easiest. This straightforward view of morality means granting others the same rights we grant ourselves — and granting ourselves the same rights as others! It is a pragmatic stance, in which values are relative and dependent on the way each person thinks, as long as they fully respect the rule of reciprocity[18]. Virtue will be the privilege of the fair, those who are neither selfish nor generous. The only (and very important) assertion I have made is that the generous, who recognise the rights of others all too well, should not deny themselves equal rights. **It is not valid to tilt the scales in either direction, not even if we are on the losing end.**

This is much more easily said than done. The person must really want to renounce their mode of behaviour because they believe it is inadequate and ineffective. They need to be absolutely convinced they want to walk the path of fairness, in spite of the internal and external obstacles they will inevitably run into. Next, they will have to start to put it into practice. But how does one make such a great change? It seems simple, especially for the generous, who can only gain from it. However, because their vanity and self-esteem are entirely tied up with the idea of self-sacrifice, their first feelings will be negative, of debasement.

This feeling that one's value has been diminished is very strong and may feel like an almost insurmountable obstacle. This happens mostly because the generous live in a context that works to reinforce their habitual conduct. Those around them will make critical, depreciative comments, as if their behaviour was unrecognisable. For someone who is taking their first steps in this new direction, negative observations can be enough to halt the evolutionary process they have so seriously embarked upon. **This is, in fact, the path to overcoming our second big obstacle in life (undue guilt), which is even more difficult to overcome than the first (tolerating frustration).**

18 Although I am no expert on the work of the American pragmatists, I am partial to what I have read by philosopher Richard Rorty on the importance of substituting hope for knowledge; on the capital importance of action; and accepting that we live in an ever-changing world. Rorty argues for "the priority of the need to create new ways of being human, and a new heaven and a new earth for these new humans to inhabit" ("Ethics Without Principles", in *Philosophy and Social Hope*, 1994). I am enchanted by the idea that each generation and era must revisit its values, and that the facts must speak louder than anything. At the same time, I believe it is essential that this be done without cynicism and without renouncing solidarity and respect for the social relations we have come to defend.

twenty six

At this stage, in which the process is already under-way and the individuals are viscerally longing for drastic change, the generous often receive the help of an unexpected, surprising phenomenon: romantic love! They fall in love with someone very similar to themselves. Obviously, at this stage it wouldn't make the slightest sense to fall for someone selfish, which probably occurred in the past due to their dissatisfaction with themselves. They may still not be entirely at peace with themselves, but they certainly no longer admire the selfish, of whom they want to rid themselves for once and for all.

Romantic love is very intense and is accompanied by a great deal of fear — a curious, unexpected ingredient[19]. This mixture of total fascination for the loved one, the feeling of plenitude that their presence brings, plus a strong, often vague feeling of fear, is what we call passion. It often takes place in complex situations, in which, for example, the lovers are married to other people — and their partners are incompatible.

I have written about love so many times that it is amazing I can still find something new to say about it. In this text, the protagonist isn't love, but guilt, which can play an important role. Let's take a closer look at how the emotional events in the previous example, involving lovers married to other people, play out. As the weeks go by and the relationship develops, certain initial problems are solved — among which the male sexual difficulties typical of this phase of romantic love. Other initial fears also diminish, especially those related to the loss of one's individuality, the fear that we might be "diluted" by the other, drawn underwater by their charms — a fear which leads Ulysses, in Homer's *Odyssey*, to have himself tied to the ship's mast when they sail through the sea of sirens. The couple starts to make the plans typical of those in love. They begin to think about a life in common, in which they would be happy if they could be together all the time.

At this point in the story, and with total clarity, the biggest dilemma arises: to look after oneself and preserve the loving relationship so yearned for, or give it up for the wife/husband and children. Will they be able to overcome their feeling of guilt for the suffering they will cause others? Will they be able to resist the pressures and blackmail to which they will be subjected on the path to forming a new couple? What is the "weight" of love and what is the "weight" of one's duties? What is worth more: love or family?

The generous are now faced with an enormous problem, perhaps the biggest of all, since it is divided between two feelings of the greatest importance, both highly valued by the generous and by society: love and guilt. Additionally, they may think they are doing their family unfair damage, even though the selfish spouse has become intolerable company, which is what led to the waning of their feelings in the first place. But what about the kids? What is best for them? I don't want to go into these issues, because, as I have said before, everything can and should be seen as relative. Each person will have their own answer to the above questions, which will depend on their personal convictions — and there is no one correct answer to these terrible existential dilemmas. What really remains to be seen here is whether a person who believes they have the moral right to fight for their emotional happiness is able to overcome their greatest enemy: guilt.

Perhaps we should start at the end: the great majority of loving couples who find themselves in the situation I have described do not end up together. In other words, love does not win, although it is an important ally in the battle against guilt. What happens is that guilt also receives strong reinforcement, and the issue of children is very important to most people. One form of reinforcement is public opinion, which tends to be conservative even today — especially among older people, parents and close relatives, as well as the couple's friends, oft times scared by the possibility of similar problems in their own future. The other reinforcement, which I have already mentioned, is the mechanism I call fear of happiness. The situation provokes a vague fear that haunts us like a ghost, promising imminent tragedy when we experience a happiness never felt before. Because our happiness when we are with someone we love is very intense, our fear takes on the same magnitude, which fuels the urge to free ourselves precisely of that which does us so much good. It is paradoxical, but that is what we are like.

I think being fully aware of the fear of happiness and its power is the key to unravelling this confusion. I believe it is the most important factor, more than the weight of public opinion and even guilt. Love is, in these cases, so strong that guilt alone is not enough to prevent its consummation. Obviously, those who renounce this love miss the historic opportunity to start a revolution in their lives.

As such, I think the revolutionary potential of romantic love is something very intense indeed, which justifies the way it has been worshipped in poetry and prose. Sentimentally happy couples become much more self-sufficient and less reliant on the approval of others, essentially depending only on each other's assessment. Happy couples become freer of material ambitions, and their romantic dream may even include a discreet house in some far-flung place, far from the crowds and rather superficial values that define the dreams of the majority. Their fundamental fuel becomes spiritual in nature, both living the "almost uterine" serenity afforded by their loved one's presence.

19 Love is perhaps the emotion to which I have most devoted myself professionally. Early on I realized that passion was associated with an intense, good-quality emotional bond, as well as great fear. I used to see this fear, in spite of the fact that it was always present, as something unexpected, at least from an intellectual point of view. Even today few people realize that intense love provokes fear. After all, it is one of the biggest dreams — if not the biggest — of most people.

To this day, love still belongs more to popular imagination than to everyday life. Even in literature and cinema, the lovers almost always separate at the end. We are obliged to acknowledge that there is a lot of antagonism to love in our subjectivity — and it is sometimes reinforced by real external obstacles. Some decades ago, I identified this fear of love. In more recent times I have named the set of ingredients that define this dramatic inner hurdle as the "antilove factor". It is composed of at least three factors, which I have mentioned in another footnote and which I will state again: the fear of future suffering related to the possible loss of one's romantic partner; and the enormous fear of losing oneself in the other, of becoming diluted, dependent, and depersonalized in their presence. The third and most important ingredient is the fear that happiness itself causes us; that is, it seems that when we feel very happy, we increase our chances of running into disaster. Even when we don't, this is how we feel and the way we feel informs the way we act. We go about trying to free ourselves of the situation responsible for our happiness, personally destroying what we most value. Here lies, in my opinion, the self-destructive impulse that everyone has to a different degree. We must stay alert to it and be very cautious about this fear of happiness and the destruction it can cause. I don't believe there is a solution for this process, which, in my understanding, is deeply and intimately linked to our existence. Like everything without a solution, all we can do is use our reason as much as possible in order to keep these processes in check and minimize any destructive tendencies. I believe that simply knowing these processes exist makes it possible to defend ourselves from them to a degree. Those who know that fear of happiness exists may be able to avoid fleeing a healthy relationship. Those who do not run away will not be disappointed, because fear of happiness tends to wane as time goes by.

twenty seven

It's a shame that all kinds of internal and external pressures end up getting in the way of this romantic objective, which, if adhered to by a significant number of couples, could bring about important changes in our social structures. My clinical experience, accompanying hundreds of loving couples, has shown me that more than 95% of them don't end up together, which is a shame, both for them and in terms of any hope we may have for moral advancement in the private and social spheres. **In addition to the internal pressures I have already mentioned, I would like to add yet another: the difficulty we have living life more lightly, without conflicts and challenges. It's as if we dream of uterine harmony, but get quickly bored when we are living in a way that resembles it. We dream of peace, but grow so accustomed to upheavals that anything different requires great adaptation and a long, painful transition.** For this reason, we often prefer to leave things as they are rather than take on so many little-known obstacles capable of generating new suffering. I will return to this subject shortly.

External pressures include all manner of temptations related to other people's material assets and lifestyles. It is hard to turn one's back on the seductive and glam-

orous pleasures that modern societies, rich with new consumer items, insist on offering. It is hard to give up travel, adornments, erotic seduction, and so many other things in favour of an almost monastic life centred on love and intellectual pleasures, even when shared with an ideal companion. Not to mention working environments, where we are not in full control of our own destiny and any slip can bring about the loss of our means of survival, the basic things we need for a decent lifestyle.

So, what am I saying? That, in practice, even the few couples who accomplish the extraordinary feat of overcoming the powerful forces resulting from the alliance of guilt, external pressures, and fear of happiness end up giving in and going back to living much as they did before. Generosity in the most intimate relationships inevitably comes undone, since the union of two very similar people means that both must give and receive. This kind of intimate exchange helps build a relationship founded on fairness, mutual respect, and genuine concern for one another. This kind of relationship is rich and comforting, but is usually restricted to family, extending, obviously, to children, who will benefit enormously from this sort of environment.

The process runs aground in the sphere of social relations and their inability to maintain the revolutionary possibilities of love in its early stages. Couples who live in harmony end up giving in to the above-mentioned pressures and rarely manage to be any different to other couples as regards the social world. They ad-

Flávio Gikovate

here to the consumerist materialism typical of our culture, and unnecessarily, since it offers so little. What's more, perhaps because they feel guilty about being happier than most in their marital relationships, they tend to reconstruct a pattern of social conduct typical of the generous; always ready to help the less fortunate, even if this help is uncalled for, giving rise to envy and reigniting the negative processes I have described.

This is what currently happens, but it doesn't mean they can't evolve in the near future, seeing as the most difficult part has already been done. These people live in a fair environment at home and, little by little, may start to feel less guilty about the great privilege they have attained, which inspires undue guilt and inappropriately generous behaviour. When they are able to take this second, even more difficult step forward (or at least keep it going longer, since it isn't rare in the early stages of happy relationships), they will interrupt this tendency to be overly generous with those around them and will stop repeating the pattern they have managed to abandon in their intimate lives. I believe that an increase in the number of people successful in love will help this situation; the privileged will they are feel less of an exception and freer to live their privilege without as much guilt. It is worth fighting to establish solid, consistent intimate relationships; they have great revolutionary potential and have been the main inspiration of my work over the last thirty years.

twenty eight

The path to fulfilment in love is not the only one capable of tipping one's inner scales in favour of fair behaviour — which is attained through the victory of reason over guilt. In general, it is hard for people to achieve the condition they so yearn for even when they are totally committed to it. **In intimate relationships, a dilemma is born, leading individuals to put their personal rights before their partner's desires. Even when one doesn't have this kind of dilemma, it may still be easier if they better understand how vanity works: the enormous obstacles we face are often insidiously reinforced by vanity.** If such obstacles were not so difficult to overcome, many of us would have already managed to do so and we would be living fairly in a reasonable world.

I have already said that in today's appearance-worshipping consumer societies it takes a great deal of inner strength not to give in to temptation. We must fight the almost inevitable urge to (when we can afford it) buy beautiful new cars, the brand-name handbag that "everyone who matters" has, piles of clothes, beauty products, etc. Not to mention the surgical and other resources that can take away the "tired look" that the years impose on us.

Flávio Gikovate

All it takes is a brief period of lower self-esteem (when we are discontent with ourselves and our behaviour, which happens from time to time) **to make us give in to the temptation to give ourselves some of these seductive consumer items. Our vanity is boosted again and we feel a peculiar erotic stirring, which is very pleasant and, unfortunately, doesn't last very long. What happens? We yearn for repetition, for similar sensations, all of which are short-lived and thus require further repetition. As addicts, we chase after a sense of wellbeing to attenuate our momentary drop in self-esteem.**

The worst part starts here: our self-esteem is damaged even further by our actions — giving in to the very ephemeral pleasures of which we are so critical, because we know they are shallow and take us nowhere. We feel bad because we are acting like "everyone else" — we who have managed to build (or perhaps not because we deserve it, but through favourable coincidences) a lifestyle more consistent with and founded on solid values. Our self-image starts to slide, bringing greater fragility and a higher tendency to consumerism, which fuels our vanity and worsens our self-esteem. In this case, vanity and self-esteem stand in opposition to one another.

We might seem OK on the outside, but on the inside... In this case our addiction is not only being reinforced, but it is also becoming more and more difficult to defeat. Here we have fair people living exactly like everyone else and who cannot be distinguished from the majority. The selfish, the generous and the fair (rare in our society) cannot be told apart. Obviously, if we are able to make this observation they cannot be referred to as fair, since they lead public lives that are very different to their private ones. **Many of those blessed with the strength and determination to turn their personal lives upside down lose the vigour and revolutionary potential of romantic love in moments of weakness. They regress to old behaviours. They go back to being like "everyone else". Vanity has won out over our ideals.**

Vanity is our greatest challenge, and we have to find a way not to be slaves to it. Even if we are unable to free ourselves of vanity, because it is an integral part of our sexual instinct, we have to find a way to subjugate it to reason. We must take great care, because it is not uncommon for the process to be inverted and before we know it we are in its grips again. We need to be careful not to let ourselves be irremediably sucked into it.

twenty nine

At least theoretically, the clear, decisive awareness that we wish to reach a point of fairness (which would indicate that we have fully evolved morally and emotionally) should lead us, over time, in this direction. I believe this. I also believe that one of our greatest stumbling blocks is the fact that we have many flawed ideas. That is, beautiful false ideas can only lead to new mistakes. False ideas lead us down the wrong paths and bring frustrating results. Many people thus conclude that having the right ideas is not enough. I agree that we shouldn't underestimate how hard it is to achieve our goals, but I don't think the fact that we haven't achieved them means our ideas are not consistent. I don't share the view that beautiful ideas are correct in principle, and that their lack of concretization is due to subtle, often unconscious, psychological processes that should be worked to exhaustion so as to allow such ideas to finally rein. I do not belong to the kingdom of ideas, but of facts.

If I am right in my assertion that fairness is true moral evolution (rather than sinking further into the domain of generosity), it will be attained by a growing number of people with this awareness. It will bring palpable results on an intellectual level, in which inner satisfaction and increased self-esteem will indicate that people are truly on the path to solid evolution.

I reaffirm my point of view that a concrete dilemma, something that urges us toward the change we desire (as is the case with romantic love, which stands in opposition to old values that are no longer satisfactory), can help us shake off our inertia and react quicker. A serious illness can also inspire in us the right to chase goals, material or personal, that we previously considered futile or unnecessary. With the phantom of death looming in front of us, or faced with great suffering, we may find the inner strength to change what should ideally be motivated only by our convictions and common sense. It is sad to think that we are only capable of granting ourselves certain rights when we know death is lurking nearby! It would be nice if we could begin the process of change without this. What's more, we must take care not to go back to our old patterns of behaviour as soon as the danger has passed.

Feelings of guilt (always stimulated by the selfish), **the fear of direct or indirect reprisal** (including the fear of happiness), **and vanity** (which is always seeking ways to stand out from the crowd) **work together against any intellectual predisposition that may help us attain an impartial, fair moral standing. On the one hand is reason; on the other, all the strong emotions and feelings underpinning the ideas behind flawed traditional attitudes.** The dispute begins when our reason starts acting clearly, vehemently, and consistently. Any error in the positioning of our reason is enough to allow our feelings to win, which leads to the perpetuation of known patterns. **Solid ideas have revolutionary potential, whereas emotions play a conservative role!**

This justifies the case for reason I have been making for over thirty years. I have never understood human beings as a territory of conscious and unconscious battles between drives, different forces, introjected paternal figures, etc., in which reason is a passive spectator. I don't believe that the instinctive forces that dictate the behaviour of other mammals should have similar importance in human beings. We have them, of course. But we also have reason, which radically distinguishes and differentiates us, makes us conscious of our condition, makes us responsible, capable of building social structures that are not governed purely by the laws of the jungle, capable too of building a system of values to guide us even when they stand in opposition to our instinctive impulses and other emotional forces.

I don't underestimate emotions. I also don't underestimate reason, the privileged equipment that we don't use well most of the time — because it is contaminated with emotions that lead us to hatch flawed ideas. I believe that increasingly accurate reflection, the assessment of our own experiences and those of the people around us — as well as other psychological processes that we don't always know how to describe and which are part of what we call intuition — can

generate ever-more substantial ideas, some of which can occasion important advances. Sometimes simple, obvious conclusions can lead to great steps forward. They may take a while to happen, precisely because they encounter opposition in our feelings and the difficult process of breaking with our beliefs (thoughts that appear to be ours but were really handed down, ready-made, from previous generations).

I think the idea that fairness should take precedence over generosity is a simple, obvious conclusion in moral terms. It shifts the emphasis away from the extremes so loved by vanity and propels us in the opposite direction, toward moderation. This new posture, if accepted and put into practice, "merely" means a new point of equilibrium from a moral point of view. But it has important and dramatic consequences, because instead of the dualism of selfishness-generosity, we begin to live the unicity of fairness.

At the end of the day, is a fair person "good" or "evil?" I don't think it is useful to consider fairness as "good". It would, in a sense, only recreate the old dualism, in which unfairness would be equated with "evil". I prefer to leave things like this: "evil" is selfishness; "good" is generosity; and fairness is fairness. Both "good" and "evil" are unfair!

30 thirty

What are the characteristics of the fair? What are they like? We already know that they are people who actually grant themselves and others equal rights and obligations. Since there are very few people like this, it is hard to describe them accurately. It's as if we didn't have a photo of the fair. Perhaps we can get an "identikit drawing", an idea of what we imagine they are like. **I believe that, as in the moral arena, the fair tend to be balanced in other aspects of life; i.e. they are hard-working, but allow themselves plenty of free time for personal pursuits — which can vary, because they too are different from one another. They are tolerant of differences, but, when in the role of leader, they are as demanding of others as they are of themselves, respecting, obviously, individual differences. They are tactful and polite, but do not make undue concessions in order to be loved. In fact, I imagine the fair as much more emotionally independent, undoubtedly better equipped to be alone than the selfish and the generous.**

The proposed moral advancement will usher in corresponding emotional development. People's love lives will probably change considerably, because those who are OK on their own become more demanding, only get into relationships based on affinities and are radical defenders of individual rights[20]. What is really hard to predict is what the fair will be like with respect to sexuality: will they want to associate it with love or will they take a simpler, freer approach to sex? Will sex figure among the serious aspects of life or will it be simply recreational? I don't have the answer. All I know is that sex won't be what it is today, a subtle manifestation of hostility between the sexes (or people) and part of the terrible game of power and domination between the selfish and the generous.

I don't want to venture too far into suppositions to divine what fair human beings will be like, because I don't want to lose touch with reality. Whenever this happens, errors tend to multiply. It won't be my task to study the behaviour of the fair, since I don't believe big advances in behaviour are possible in the short term. We may come to know a growing number of fair people, who are now very rare. They may come as much from the ranks of the selfish, thanks to undeniable advances, as from the generous, because of advances that will seem like retrogression to them. This is difficult for both personality types, because the process depends on rupture, breaking with the patterns that govern them. It is very hard to change anything in our subjectivity, but, regardless of our differences, I believe that evolution is possible for both the selfish and the generous.

One thing strikes me as clear and highly relevant: since the fair will be happy with their behaviour, their

self-esteem will be good. This is why fairness will be a difficult condition to achieve, but it will be stable and solid once attained. I think the fair will leave this state only for very strong reasons, and even then not for long. In practice, this means that the fair will have much more control over their vanity, which is more active when we experience a decrease in self-esteem. Vanity will never leave us completely, and this is a good thing, because it is responsible (at least partially) for our defences. When we are subtly offended or humiliated, it is what signals to us that we are in an unfavourable situation, allowing us to improve our positioning in relation to other people and situations.

Vanity, however, is responsible for our tendency to radicalize all manner of things, since it feeds on distinction and this comes easily when we behave extravagantly, or eccentrically — literally, not positioned centrally or on an axis. All excesses are manifestations of vanity: body-worship, exaggerated consumerism or a radical renouncement of it, ambitions to attain greater social or intellectual status or power. Radicalizations run down everything in their path, even when motivated by the most beautiful ideas. Vanity aggravates competition (which is dangerous even when fair), which distances people from one another, turning them into opponents, enemies, competitors, rivals, objects of envy — and how common all of these feelings are!

Vanity also brings about a radicalization of generosity, increasing the "good" actions that give rise to

more and more "bad" ones, whence my conviction that "good" and "bad" are two faces of unfairness. Vanity demands to be fed at any cost, which is a remedy for low self-esteem. Distinction implies that one has attained conditions only accessible to a small number of people. Vanity clamours for extraordinary beauty, extraordinary wealth, extraordinary learning, extraordinary generosity and self-sacrifice. It demands and promises a kind of pleasure that I call aristocratic.

Aristocratic pleasure condemns most people to unhappiness. Wealth is only a reason for distinction because it is distributed unevenly, favouring a minority. When beauty is overly valued, it condemns most people to unhappiness. The same is true of learning and a person's ability to give more and more, or to take what isn't theirs in a radical, presumptuous way.

---

20 Most people have a negative response to the term "individualism" because it is used as a synonym for selfishness, which doesn't make any sense, since the selfish generally like groups precisely because this is where they can find someone to feed off like a parasite. Individualism has come about as a result of the technological advances I have already mentioned and has given rise to important changes in the outlook and behaviour of a whole new generation, which, indirectly, has also influenced older members of society. Individualism is actually an important acquisition: a greater ability to be on one's own, even if because of the availability of an enormous range of interesting, individual activities.

Individualism has brought big changes in the way in which people relate to one another in their love lives and the institution of marriage. For example, nowadays there are many married couples who sleep in separate rooms because they have incompatible sleeping habits. In the past, couples who slept in separate rooms were

▸

seen in a negative light: it was supposed that they were going through a serious crisis in their relationship or even in the process of separating. People's ability to make concessions has also dropped off considerably, since they are becoming less and less necessary.

A married person can now go to the cinema or visit friends and relatives on their own without it being interpreted as a sign that they are about to get divorced. As a result, instead of always making concessions, a couple no longer need spend all of their time together, which creates a new lifestyle and romanticism, which is much more respectful of individual preferences. The days are numbered for the romantic ideal of the 19th and much of the 20th century: fusion — precisely the kind of relationship that provokes fear due to its demanding nature. People are now tending away from this. Instead of two halves, they now see themselves as wholes (in spite of a certain feeling of incompleteness), and seek closeness, rather than fusion with their partners. I call this closeness of two wholes "+love", more than love, something along the lines of friendship, companionship. This kind of alliance is much less threatening to one's individuality and more compatible with the reality of today's world.

As well as helping solve dilemmas in our love lives, I think individualism makes a decisive contribution to solving the selfishness–generosity duality. Therefore, I see it as one of the most important achievements of our era, something that can bring very positive benefits if understood as part of the process that frees us and strengthens us internally. More self-sufficient people rarely involve themselves in the dynamics of domination that have characterized more traditional relationships to date.

In the family contexts of times past, we never attained a degree of identity and individuality similar to that which we can have today. A patriarchal approach to bringing up new generations strikes me as completely senseless. It isn't that we lived in solidary alliances and now we live alone. We lived in a regime of tyranny that has started to crumble as a result of individualism. Other beliefs have also crumbled and we are living through a period of disorientation and lack of direction. This shouldn't be blamed on individualism, however, but on fast technological development, which has bowled us over with an avalanche of new consumer products that we have yet to learn to deal with adequately.

thirty one

What happens to fairness? Although it may presently seem hard to achieve in our intimate and social relationships, once the path has been discovered, fair behaviour is accessible to all. One person's excessive generosity necessarily implies the selfishness of others. But the fair don't condemn anyone to unfairness! There is room for everyone in fairness, which definitely isn't the case with generosity. As such, fairness is part of the pleasure — or inner satisfaction that generates good self-esteem — that can be called "democratic", that is, accessible to all. If we are able to value democratic pleasures, we will bring about an important improvement in our interpersonal relationships, since envy and competition are inexorably much smaller.

It is also clear to me that vanity is a great enemy of democratic pleasures. How can we distinguish ourselves for the possession of something that others also have or may come to have? Perhaps this is one of the reasons why we fight so little for satisfactions that don't distinguish us in any way, although they may represent some of our greatest sources of happiness. Another democratic pleasure is love, because the fact that we are emotionally happy doesn't reduce the chances of other couples also being happy. The same applies to love of the arts, knowledge, non-competitive sports; so many simple things, accessible to everyone and to which we devote ourselves so little.

In practice, we give up almost all important, democratic pleasures for the aristocratic distinction that vanity demands. We cannot go on underestimating the importance of this process. We cannot position ourselves against vanity, even knowing that it is inherent to our sexual instinct and that we will never be totally free of it, but it doesn't need to have the importance it has acquired in our personal and collective lives. Our social order and private lives needn't be so submissive to it. It is ludicrous to renounce everything that is essential and reasonable just to try and feel special physically, financially, or intellectually. There must be a more consistent kind of existence than this. It should be possible to feel good for trying to lead a fair life founded on balanced intimate relationships, and which is professionally satisfying but not overly competitive.

No emotion or feeling stemming from our instincts — or that has been reinforced by the beliefs we all inherit and which have an almost biological solidity — **disappears just because we are rationally opposed to it. Nothing (whether hate, jealousy, or love) is so obedient. Much less vanity. However, the reinforcement of reason greatly increases the influence of a feeling and the opposition of reason tends to attenuate it.** When we believe that jealousy is an integral and inexorable part of love (and even an indication of its intensity) and accept it without reservation, we become more possessive and jealous than when we stand in opposition to it. Jealousy won't disappear, but it will be, at least in part, controlled by reason, which will gradually weaken it. I believe the same to be true of vanity and its relatives: competitiveness, ambition, and the radicalization of all manner of moral and intellectual positions.

I think that once the initial pain has subsided, when we give up the ephemeral pleasures of life (so ephemeral they are always demanding new and renewed distinction), we find ourselves faced with far more stable, solid pleasures. I think it is worth setting aside our vanity — at least, as much as possible — to better enjoy the pleasures of self-esteem, solid relationships and friendships, stable bonds even with our material possessions of real value (home, objects inherited from people we love, a favourite pen, watch, books, CDs, etc.), as well as a moral posture truly committed to fairness. Our self-esteem will most probably grow when we are able to position ourselves in a similar manner to the one I have described. I repeat: we are looking at an "identikit drawing" of something we may begin to approach if we are able to move toward fairness.

Fair individuals who have their vanity under control don't consider themselves saviours, heroes who are going to free their people from the atrocities of tyrants (who, if successful, and if they aren't careful, end up much like those they fought so hard to defeat). Rather,

they are participants, worthy members of the community they live in. They want to live in a socially useful way and expect due compensation for their efforts.
They are not always competing, nor do they wallow in
the hatred born of envy. They can live in peace and be
proud of the worthy life they lead.

32 thirty two

But will we be able to deal with it? It seems so good, so simple, and even easier to achieve than the success that so many of us struggle toward and rarely find. What I have described is someone who is "already there", but it seems people really prefer (or only know how) to "chase after" their goals. That is, it seems easy to reach a state of serenity, inner harmony, and a worthy and reasonable lifestyle, but people don't really know how to deal with it because it ushers in a certain depression and feeling of emptiness. It is as if life, full of meaning and palpable gratifications, suddenly makes no sense.

We need to take stock before setting forth in this area of utmost importance in the process of becoming happier. As we learn to live we are strongly influenced by our social environment. Not everyone has such a hard a time enjoying the serenity I have described. People who grew up in small towns, as long as they have reasonable quality of life and haven't been overly contaminated by information about an apparently much more interesting lifestyle (now rare due to the far reach of mass communications), most likely have different psychological processes to our own and are